M000086263

BETHLEHEM'S

Lamb

*Discover the true meaning of
the first Christmas*

CREATION HOUSE

BETHLEHEM'S

Lamb

Discover the true meaning of
the first Christmas

SANDY DAVIS KIRK

BETHLEHEM'S LAMB by Dr. Sandy Davis Kirk
Published by Creation House Books
A Charisma Media Company
600 Rinehart Road
Lake Mary, Florida 32746
www.charismamedia.com

Unless otherwise noted, all Scripture quotations are from the Holy Bible, New International Version. Copyright © 1973, 1978, 1984, International Bible Society. Used by permission.

Scripture quotations marked KJV are from the King James Version of the Bible.

Scripture quotations marked NKJV are from the New King James Version of the Bible. Copyright © 1979, 1980, 1982 by Thomas Nelson, Inc., publishers. Used by permission.

Design Director: Bill Johnson
Cover design by Nancy Panaccione

Visit the author's website: www.gloryofthelamb.com

Library of Congress Cataloging-in-Publication Data:
2011928575
International Standard Book Number: 978-1-61638-588-0

First edition

11 12 13 14 15 — 9 8 7 6 5 4 3 2 1
Printed in Canada

For God so loved the world that he gave his one and only Son, that whoever believes in him shall not perish but have eternal life.

—John 3:16

CONTENTS

REDISCOVERING THE GLORY OF CHRISTMAS

The Greatest Love Story Ever Told

THE STORY OF the first Christmas resonates with deep human emotions pulsing beneath the surface of the narrative. To rekindle the glory of Christmas in our hearts, let's take a fresh look at this greatest love story of all time.[1] But this time, let's step inside the story to feel these raw human feelings.

The story springs to life when we feel Mary's awestruck wonder at the presence of the angel, shimmering in living light. But let's feel her deep love for Joseph and her dread of telling him, "I am with child!"[2] Then let's sense Joseph's wounded love and the turmoil and rage he would have experienced. And when he learns the truth about the baby in a dream, let's run with him sobbing to Mary's house as he begs her forgiveness. These are poignant human emotions and real life experiences with which we can identify.

Let's further imagine the bitter shame of Mary's parents when they hear that their own daughter is pregnant and unwed. But let's rejoice with them as they finally realize—their first grandchild will be the Son of God!

Let's peer into the animal stable, filled with urine-soaked hay, and watch Joseph, feeling desperately inadequate, trying to comfort Mary in the throes of childbirth. But see him rise to the occasion as his trembling hands guide God's Son into the world. Then watch scraggly bearded shepherds weep like babies when they look into the face of God.

Most importantly, as we look into the story of the first Christmas, let's unwrap the stunning mystery of why God's Son had to be born in Bethlehem. Why must He be born in a stable and placed in a manger? Why were shepherds chosen, out of all the people on earth, to be the first to attend His birth?

Oh, this is the greatest love story of all time—when God's own Son shed His garments of glory to become *Bethlehem's Lamb*. In its highest sense, it's the story of a Father who tore His own Son from His embrace and gave Him to save the world: "For God so loved the world that he gave his one and only Son, that whoever believes in him shall not perish but have eternal life."[3]

So join me now as together we peel back the holiday trappings to take a fresh look at the exquisite joy and piercing pain of the greatest love story ever told. Come feel the Father's heart trembling with love for His Son until your own heart floods with His love.

Then God's love will shine in everything you do this Christmas. Your shopping will have more meaning. Your gifts will come even more from the heart. God's love bending low at Christmas will fill everything with love and tender devotion. And this season will be flooded with the glory of the first Christmas, as you behold once again the beauty of Bethlehem's Lamb.

Introduction Endnotes

1. "Without a doubt we could spend our lives searching the literature of the world for a story as beautiful as that of the Nativity and never find it," writes R. Kent Hughes, *Luke: That You May Know the Truth*, vol. 1 (Wheaton, IL: Crossway, 1998), 29.

2. The latest nativity movie depicts Mary as a girl who seems passive about her faith and can barely tolerate Joseph until the end. I believe God would have chosen a Jewish girl who yearns with aching love for her Messiah. And the Father, wanting a home of love for His Son, would have chosen a couple who are deeply in love.

3. John 3:16

Chapter 1

AN ANGEL'S PROMISE

Announcing the Coming Messiah

S HE QUIETLY SLIPS from her pallet and tiptoes up the ladder to the terrace on the roof. She leans against the stone ledge and breathes in the cool night air. The mingled fragrance of jasmine and honeysuckle, climbing up the outer wall and draping over the edge of the balcony, drifts through the atmosphere and fills her senses.

She wraps her prayer shawl, which Joseph had given her at their betrothal, around her shoulders. Sighing heavily, she thinks of her beloved. Although Joseph is several years older, she has admired him for as long as she can remember, so strong and handsome, with godly character beyond the other young men of Nazareth. She feels faint with love as she thinks of the one who holds her heart.

He has loved her too. Pretending not to notice her striking beauty, his heart had been captivated by her pure, loving, gentle nature, and most of all her passion for God. Patiently he had

5

waited for the day he could ask her father to allow her to become his betrothed.

Her face flushes and she smiles as she recalls their day of betrothal. Joseph, so nervous and shy, had lavished her with gifts. Then, before the rabbi, their families, and their God, he held her hands and promised to protect and love her forever.

With her heart bursting with happiness, she hugs her prayer shawl more tightly and looks up to heaven. Bright stars splayed across the black velvet backdrop of the sky sparkle like diamonds overhead. She lifts her heart in prayer and her soul floods with longing for God. For there is Someone even more dear to her than Joseph. Mary's heart aches for her Messiah.

> *Oh, Father, when will our Messiah come? When will it happen? We have waited so long. Our people are oppressed. We need a Savior. But most of all, Father, we need our Messiah, The Anointed One, The Christ. Oh, God, my heart yearns for my Messiah!*

Then a thought, which she has kept silently locked in the vault of her heart, rises to her consciousness. *Oh, if only I could be the one honored to carry the promised Messiah and birth Him to this world!* she dares to think, for every Jewish maiden of her day hopes she will be chosen to bring the Messiah into the world. *If only Joseph and I could be the chosen ones.*

Suddenly, without any warning she hears a voice behind her. "Mary," the voice says in warm, rich, heavenly tones. Startled, she leaps to her feet and wheels around to discover the source of the voice. As she turns, bolts of light strike her eyes. The brightness pulsates with life, radiant and supernal, beyond anything she has ever seen on earth.

At first glance she shrinks back, frightened and shaking. But slowly her eyes adjust to the light until she can dimly make out a vague presence in the midst of the glory—the figure of a man enveloped in dazzling, living light.

His presence stuns this fourteen-year-old maiden. With his arms folded over his chest, he speaks with the authority of one who has come from the presence of God. His eyes flash. Sparks seem to shoot from them, penetrating Mary's heart as he speaks: "Greetings, you who are highly favored! The Lord is with you."[1]

Mary's face flushes and beads of sweat begin to run down the back of her neck. She stands trembling all over. *What could this mean?* she wonders.

Then Gabriel explains, "Do not be afraid, Mary, you have found favor with God. You will be with child and give birth to a son, and you are to give him the name Jesus."[2] "He will be great and will be called the Son of the Most High. The Lord will give him the throne of his father David, and he will reign over the house of Jacob forever; his kingdom will never end."[3]

Mary can hardly think. Her throat tightens and she can't speak. Finally, her head spinning, she manages to stammer, "How can this be…since I am a virgin?"[4] Suddenly, the words of Isaiah the prophet flash before her: "The virgin will be with child and give birth to a son."[5] *Could this be me?* she marvels, *Since I am a virgin?*

With wide eyes she gazes at the angel, her face deeply troubled. What the angel says next is a mystery too fathomless to fully comprehend: "The Holy Spirit will come upon you, and the power of the Most High will overshadow you. So the Holy One to be born will be called the Son of God."[6]

Mary's heart almost stops. *The Son of God!* she thinks, biting her quivering lip. With her mind still swirling, the angel continues, "Even Elizabeth your relative is going to have a child in her old age, and she who was said to be barren is in her sixth month."[7]

Elizabeth? she thinks with a sudden gasp. *How can that be, for she is long past the age of child bearing?* But the angel interrupts her thoughts with these stunning words of faith: "For nothing is impossible with God."[8]

When Mary hears these words, though she doesn't understand, she humbly bows her head and whispers, "I am the Lord's servant…May it be to me as you have said."[9]

Then as quickly as he came, the angel disappears. She rubs her eyes and ponders all the angel has said. *This must mean that God has chosen me to bear the Messiah! The Son of God will be conceived in my womb! Oh, God, this is too much for me to comprehend…*[10]

Excitement fills her as she mumbles out loud, "I can hardly wait to tell Joseph! He will be so proud to be the earthly father of the Messiah!" But then, slowly and imperceptibly, a dreadful thought forms in the back of her mind and crowds its way into her consciousness: *What if Joseph doesn't understand? What will he think when I become pregnant?*

Fear creeps coldly up her spine. *Will he think I've been with another man? Will he believe me when I tell him the child is fathered by God?* These thoughts reel through her mind, causing her fears to mount. Her mouth runs dry as she considers the worst possible outcome. *Will he reject me? Will he divorce me, which is the only way betrothal can be broken?*[11] *Will he have me stoned for adultery?*

> *Oh, God, please let Joseph understand. Surely he will believe me, for he too longs for our Messiah! But, Father, even if he doesn't believe me, I am willing to bear the shame for Your Son. Whatever I must suffer*

*for Him pales in comparison with the honor of carrying
the Messiah!*

With hot tears coursing down her cheeks, she cries with all
her heart,

> *Dear God, I am amazed that I have been chosen to
> carry Your Son, the Messiah, Your gift to those You
> love! I give myself to this great cause of carrying Your
> Son to the earth.*

Recalling her resolve to the angel, she lifts her hands in utter
abandonment and cries,

> *Father, here I am! I am Your servant. May it be to me
> as You have said!*

And with those words of sweet surrender, she relinquishes all
worry. Now, even as the light of the sun swallows up the light of
the stars, the afterglow of God's presence swallows up all of her
fears. She closes her eyes and drifts off to sleep on the rooftop.

And so begins God's grand love story. After thousands of years
of preparation, God has chosen a young Jewish maiden to carry
His Son. But the story doesn't begin on a rooftop of Nazareth;
it begins somewhere in eternity. It's a love story conceived in the
heart of God.

Long before He created the earth, God longed for a family.
He wanted you and me to be near Him, but there was only one
way. From the depths of eternity, God ripped open His heart
and gave us His Son as a Lamb. That's what makes this more

than a human love story. It's the story of the love of a Father for His Son. It's the story of God's love for you and me. It's the story of a Father who wrenched from His side the dearest One to His heart, and gave Him as Bethlehem's Lamb.

Chapter 1 Endnotes

1. Luke 1:28
2. Luke 1:30–31. "Thus far, Gabriel had told her nothing of his mission. But now came the Annunciation itself, and the initial words were shocking" (Hughes, *Luke*, vol. 1, 33).
3. Luke 1:32–33
4. Luke 1:34. "Mary was not disbelieving—she was simply asking for enlightenment. The question was biological: 'God, how are you going to do this?'" (Hughes, *Luke*, vol. 1, 34).
5. Isaiah 7:14
6. Luke 1:35
7. Luke 1:36
8. Luke 1:37
9. Luke 1:38
10. Mary is to be respected but not venerated. Some hold the view that she is sinless, without original sin. "That doctrine is a sad, totally unjustified distortion. Mary would have been scandalized at the thought….[However] just because others have thought too much of her, we must not imagine that our Lord is pleased when we think too little of her" (Hughes, *Luke*, vol. 1, 32).

11. Betrothal can only be broken through filing papers of divorce; and if adultery is the cause, the law required that the person who sinned must be stoned to death. However, this action was rarely taken in New Testament times.

Chapter 2

MIDNIGHT GLORY

The Conception of God the Son

M ARY, MARY, WHERE are you, child?"

Rubbing her eyes, she awakens with a start. She bolts down the ladder. "I'm sorry, Mother. I fell asleep on the terrace last night—praying." Then she halts and catches her breath as she remembers…

The memory of last night's encounter with the angel bursts over her conscious mind. Even as she remembers the flood of light that enveloped him, and most of all the message he brought, a rush of glory sweeps over her. Her face shines like the morning sun. "Oh, God, could it be true?" she gasps. A faraway look fills her eyes.

Her mother, Hannah, looks at her quizzically. "Mary, what's wrong with you? Your face glows like you've seen an angel."

"Mother, I have," she softly mumbles, hoping her mother doesn't hear.

"Ridiculous, child! Get your head out of the clouds. We've chores to do!"

Dutifully, Mary scurries through the house, lighting the stove and preparing the dough for the day's bread. But her thoughts are miles away.

All day Mary tenderly holds her emotions inside, her heart too full to speak. Then suddenly she remembers—Elizabeth! The angel had said, "Even Elizabeth your relative is going to have a child in her old age, and she who was said to be barren is in her sixth month."[1]

Oh, if only I could talk to Elizabeth, she thinks wistfully. *I could tell her about the angel's promise. If she is already six months with child, then surely she will understand.*

Later that evening as the lamps are lit and the bread and figs are placed on the low cut table, Mary announces, "I want to go visit Cousin Elizabeth. She is expecting a child, you know!"

"Nonsense, Elizabeth is far too old!" growls Heli, her father.[2] "What is wrong with you, child?" her mother asks, ladling out the soup.

But their daughter seems absorbed in her own secret thoughts. For days, to her mother's consternation, she walks around dazed, as though lost in another world. Every chance she can get, she steals away to pray—weeping, wondering, longing for God to come. Then late one night it happens...

After all in the household are asleep, she quietly climbs the ladder up to the roof. For a moment she pauses to look out across her beloved little town of Nazareth, nestled among the fertile fields and rich green slopes of Galilee.

From her view here on the terrace she can see the cobbled streets below, lined by torches sputtering fitfully on their poles. She watches the scented orange groves and gnarled fig trees spreading wide their branches in the light of the moon. Silvery olive leaves shimmer in the moonlight, and the feathery leaves of palms whisper in the midnight breeze.

Now, here on this same rooftop where she met the angel, she continues to pray. The ache within her rises to the surface and spills through her words:

> *Oh, Father, how I long for my Messiah! When will He come? You alone know, for the times and seasons are in Your hands; but oh, how my heart aches for my promised Redeemer. Father, will He come through me? I believed what the angel said, but I still don't…*

Suddenly, before another word could fall from her lips, she feels a mysterious light settling over her. The light intensifies with heat. It reminds her of the warmth she felt in the presence of the angel, but much more intense, so full of glory and fire. Her heart pounds wildly. Her whole body trembles.

Without any warning, a thick heavy glory descends upon her. She knows in an instant—this is the power of God flooding over her.

She catches her breath, inhaling deeply of this heavy, weighty presence. Tears swim in her eyes as glory drenches every part of her being. *Oh, my God, oh, my God!* she thinks, *This must be what the angel meant!* Gabriel had said, "The power of the Most High will overshadow you."[3]

Yes, Mary, even as the Shekinah glory of God overshadowed Moses's tabernacle in the wilderness, later David's tent on Mount Zion, and finally Solomon's Temple in Jerusalem,[4] this in a far greater sense is what is happening to you. For the day finally came when the glory lifted off the temple and rose up over the Mount of Olives into heaven, never to be seen again. Now, for almost five hundred years, the glory of God has been missing from the earth…[5]

Until tonight.

Now here in this lowly, sometimes despised town of Nazareth,[6] the glory has once again come down into the world. Not in the solemn splendor of the temple in Jerusalem, not amidst the glow of the golden candelabra or the smoky fragrance of the holy of holies—but God has come down on a poor man's rooftop in Galilee. Like the cloud of brilliance which overshadowed the tabernacle, now the glory has overshadowed a virgin, settling in the holy of holies of her womb.

Mary closes her eyes and surrenders completely to this ineffable glory. She feels engulfed, utterly suffused by the holy presence of God. It is fearful yet exquisitely wonderful at the same time. Tears rush down her face as billows of God's shining essence sweep over her.

So close is God's overshadowing presence, it is like a divine infusion as He implants a part of Himself into her. It is something holy, something beautiful—the very Seed of God imparted into her womb.

Moments pass, she doesn't know how many. But finally her heart overflows to God. Breathlessly she cries,

> *Oh, Father, can this be happening to me? Have You chosen me to carry Your own Son? Have you truly implanted Your Seed within my womb; Your Beloved Son—My Messiah—Almighty God enfleshed in a baby's skin?*

Yet, somehow she knows—the life of the Holy One inside her did not begin at conception, as the lives of other babies do. He has always been. He is the everlasting, uncreated Son of God. He has existed forever as God's eternal Lamb.[7] Now for this short span of time, He has come to earth through the womb of a virgin, to transform human hearts and bring us back to God.

Slowly now she can feel the intensity of God's glory lifting.

She takes a deep breath and opens her eyes, still sensing the afterglow of His lingering presence. Like Moses's face shined when He gazed at God's streaming glory, Mary's face beams with heaven's bliss. Thankfulness fills her heart as she thinks of the wonder of what has just taken place.

Hours pass and she tries to sleep; but it is impossible, so excited, so thrilled is she with the wonder of God's glory. She simply lies on the rooftop praying until the first gleam of dawn begins to spill across the Galilean slopes.

Rising early before anyone else stirs, she washes her face, changes her clothes, and combs her tussled hair. Her mother finds her already preparing the morning meal, her face shining with the glory of God.

"Hmmm…" Hannah breathes to herself, shaking her head and wondering.

Throughout the day, Mary holds her thoughts inside, often touching her stomach and smiling. She almost imagines she can feel the spark of life stirring within her. *Oh, if only I could see Cousin Elizabeth*, she thinks. *We could share our miracles together. I don't know if my parents and Joseph will believe me, but I know Elizabeth will understand. Oh, I pray that Joseph understands! Surely he will because he loves me and he believes in me so much.*

A few days pass and Mary feels the life of God stirring all the more within her. Already she feels the tenderness in her breasts and the queasiness in her stomach. Then one day she says, with a hint of fear trembling in her voice, "Mama, I want to invite Joseph to dinner tonight. There is something I must tell him…and you and Papa."

Hannah nods, studying her daughter warily. *Something is wrong, dreadfully wrong*, she thinks—a mother knows these things.

That night, after the children are dismissed and the dishes

removed from the table, Mary clears her throat and says shakily, "I have something to tell you..." She swallows hard against the emotion filling her. Joseph leans forward, eager to receive whatever news his beloved bears. Mary steals a quick glance at Joseph, and tries to steady her nerves.

She can hardly breathe past the tightness in her chest as she prepares to break the staggering news to those she loves. Her heart hammers with heavy beats. Her eyes are moist and her face flushed as she says bravely, "I am with child! The Lord has chosen me to carry His Son, the Messiah of Israel!"

Mary's words strike Joseph squarely in the chest, piercing his heart to the core. His face pales. His stomach drops. His hands clench into fists.

"No-oo!" cries Hannah, bursting into tears and burying her face in her apron. Her father looks at her incredulously. "Impossible," he groans, shaking his head. "Not my innocent little girl. Not my Mary..." Then, his face reddening, he turns to Joseph and snarls, "How could you violate my daughter?"

Joseph's eyes narrow coldly. Heat rises in his face. His vision blurs. He barely hears Heli's accusation. "W-who is the father?" he asks numbly, his voice shaking with wounded love.

Mary's eyes fill with tears. She rushes to his side and grabs his hands, tears running unchecked down her cheeks. "Joseph, I would never be unfaithful to you! You are the only man I have ever loved. Please believe me, my darling. This baby is from the Holy Spirit!"

Joseph jerks loose his hands and turns toward the door. "You expect me to believe that! What kind of fool do you take me for?" Charging out the door, he slams it behind him. He runs out into the night, blinded by tears and rage, stumbling, falling, gasping, and screaming like a mad man.

Mary plunges her face into her hands and sobs. Finally she

looks up at her father and asks softly, "You believe me, don't you Papa? Mama?" She waits for an answer, but none comes. They simply hold each other, looking down at the floor, as her mother quietly weeps.

"Then I must go see Elizabeth!" Mary says, her jaw set. "Please let me go. I know she will understand..."

"Alright, child," her father relents. "Perhaps she can speak some sense into you."

That night while tossing on her pallet, she clings desperately to the words of the angel: "You will be with child and give birth to a son, and you are to give him the name Jesus. He will be great and he will be called the Son of the Most High."[8]

The Son of the Most High...Jesus, the Messiah..., she rolls the words over and over in her mind. *I know it's true, no matter what my beloved thinks, no matter what my parents think—He is the Son of God!*

She turns over on her back and whispers,

> *Father, This is Your Son! Thank you for the great privilege of carrying the Messiah in my womb. Please give me the strength to bear the pain I must endure for Your Son. Thank You for the high honor of suffering for His sake!"*

Finally she drifts off to sleep filled with thoughts of her baby boy, the Messiah, soon to be born in the City of David as Bethlehem's Lamb.

Mary, if only you could know how your story inspires us today. You not only suffered persecution for being pregnant with the Messiah, but like the Son you carry, you are "despised and rejected"[9] by those you love the most. Just a teenage Jewish girl, yet so strong and so committed to the high calling of God in your life. I pray that we too will draw strength from Mary's courage. May you and I be encouraged to carry Jesus to a fallen world. In spite of persecution, may we be willing to endure the wounds and persevere. For "It's not about avoiding a wounded life; it's about avoiding a wasted life."[10] May we devote our lives, like Mary, to telling others, especially those we love, about the glory of Bethlehem's Lamb.

CHAPTER 2 ENDNOTES

1. Luke 1:36

2. Matthew tells us that Joseph's father is Jacob (Matt. 1:16), but Luke gives the father of Joseph as being Heli (Luke 3:23). Actually Heli was Joseph's father-in-law, Mary's father, for Luke wanted to show that Jesus is the Seed of the woman (see Genesis 3:15, KJV). (See also *Matthew Henry's Commentary, Matthew—John*, vol. V [McLean, VA: MacDonald, n.d.], 617.) Hughes makes the point that if Mary had no brothers, Mary's father Heli (in accordance with biblical tradition) would have adopted Joseph as his son (Hughes, *Luke*, vol. 1, 129).

3. Luke 1:35. The Greek of *overshadow* is *ĕpiskiazō*, meaning "to envelop in a haze of brilliancy." This is also the same word used on the Mount of Transfiguration when "a bright cloud enveloped [*ĕpiskiazō*] them" (Matt. 17:5). Again *ĕpiskiazō* is used of Peter's shadow which healed the sick: "People brought the sick into the streets and laid them on beds and mats so that at least Peter's shadow might fall on [*ĕpiskiazō*] some of them as he passed by" (Acts 5:15).

"What is described here? Certainly not a sexual union (mating) with divinity, as some have argued. Nothing so crude is suggested here. All leading scholars agree that there are no sexual overtones whatsoever....While it was not a sexual experience, it was surely a conscious experience—something Mary could feel. How could anyone have the Holy Spirit come upon him or her and be overshadowed as in the temple or on the Mount of Transfiguration and not know it?" (Hughes, *Luke*, vol. 1, 34–35).

4. Sadly, as magnificent as the glory was in Solomon's Temple, because of sin, the glory couldn't remain. Ezekiel saw the glory lift out of the temple just before the Babylonian army swept in and destroyed it in 586 B.C. (see Ezekiel 10). He watched as "the glory of the LORD went up from within the city and stopped above the mountain east of it," which was the Mount of Olives (Ezek. 11:23). When the second temple was built in 516 B.C., sometimes called Zerubbabel's Temple, the elderly people "who had seen the former temple, wept aloud" (Ezra 3:12). Why? "The chief cause of grief was that the second temple would be destitute of those things which formed the great distinguishing glory of the first; viz., the ark, the Shekinah, the Urrim and Thummim, etc. Not that this second temple was not a very grand and beautiful structure. But no matter how great its material splendor was, it was inferior in this respect to that of Solomon," says Robert Jamieson, A. R. Fausset, and David Brown, *Jamieson, Fausset, & Brown's Commentary on the Whole Bible* (Grand Rapids, MI: Zondervan, 1961), 339.

5. Later when Herod built the glorious temple on the mount in Jerusalem, which was the temple in Jesus's day, no glory rested in the holy of holies. The glory of God had departed from Israel and had not been seen on planet earth for over five hundred years. Please don't miss this point. There had been no glory on earth, not until that quiet night in Nazareth when God came down.

6. The fact that Nazareth was chosen over Jerusalem, the heart of God's work through the centuries, was shocking. "Nazareth was a 'non place.' It was not even mentioned in the Old Testament or in Josephus' writings or in the rabbinical writings....Nazareth, a shoddy, corrupt halfway stop between the port cities of Tyre and Sidon, was overrun by Gentiles and Roman soldiers....God bypassed Judea, Jerusalem, and the temple and came to a despised country, a despised town, and a humble woman" (Hughes, *Luke*, vol. 1, 29, 32).

7. The life of God's Son did not begin at conception like other babies, nor did He commence His life in Bethlehem. He has existed forever in the Triune Godhead, for something happened in the Godhead that still staggers human senses. The Son agreed to come to earth and lay down His life as a Lamb, for He "was chosen before the creation of the world" (1 Pet. 1:19–20). He is indeed God's eternal Lamb, "slain from the creation of the world" (Rev. 13:8).

8. Luke 1:31–32

9. Isaiah 53:3

10. John Piper, *Don't Waste Your Life* (Wheaton, IL: Crossway, 2003), 10.

Chapter 3

MARY'S SONG

Finding Joy in the Suffering

ITH A HEAVY heart, Mary bids farewell to her parents and joins a caravan heading south to Judea. "Papa, please tell Joseph good-bye and…and that I love him," she sighs. She can feel the tears building behind her eyes but she swallows them down until they become like a rock in her chest. She knows she will miss Joseph desperately, but she must get to Cousin Elizabeth, to someone who understands.

As the rickety cart pulls out of Nazareth, it passes the town well, where the women meet to fill their buckets with water, and especially to share the latest gossip. "Shalom, Mary," someone waves. "Where are you going?"

"I'm going to visit my cousin," she answers with a forced smile.

"What?" one of the women blurts. Then waiting until Mary is out of earshot, she whispers, "Mary is betrothed! She has no business leaving Joseph when she's supposed to be planning a wedding. Something must be wrong!"

Mary's stomach sickens, for she senses what they are saying. In fact, she knows she will be the brunt of many jokes and gossip. Indeed great rejection and misunderstanding lay ahead, but she straightens her shoulders and looks up.

Father, whatever dishonor I must endure, I thank you for the honor of carrying your Son!

As the cart rattles down the road, she lets her eyes sweep the Galilean pastures, dotted with white and yellow field lilies. As far as her eyes can see lay the olive groves and fruit orchards where lemon and orange blossoms fill the air with fragrance. She gazes on the hills and glens which once formed the backdrop of Solomon's Song. To the west she sees lovely Mount Carmel where Elijah called down fire from heaven. Beyond the western mountains stretches the Great Sea, shimmering beneath the noonday sun like a silver platter of light.

At night she shivers on the moist ground, wrapped in her prayer shawl and a woolen cloak, feeling miserable and alone. This is her first time leaving home, and the hollow ache of loneliness engulfs her as she quietly cries herself to sleep. Each morning, her stomach wretches with nausea. For almost four grueling days the sun beats mercilessly down upon her as the caravan plods toward the hill country.[1]

As they near Samaria, the caravan turns eastward, crossing over the chilling waters of the Jordan at its shallowest point. No respectable Jew would contaminate himself by walking on Samaritan ground, so they follow the east banks of the Jordan until they cross back over the river into Jericho.

Immediately after crossing the chilly waters, she sees in the distance the hills rising around Jerusalem. "We're almost there, little one," shouts the leader of the caravan. "We'll drop you off at your cousin's house in the village outside the city."

Mary's blood runs faster now. She silently prays,

> *Father, please let Elizabeth be pregnant just as the angel told me. This amazing dream will seem more real when I see my barren cousin filled with the miracle of a child. But should I tell her right away that I too am with child? Oh, please let her understand...Don't let her reject me like the others.*

The evening sun slopes gently over the Judean hills as the caravan enters the village where Zechariah and his wife, Elizabeth, live. As they near the house, the clatter of hooves on the cobbles draws Elizabeth to the window. A warm breeze blows the curtain across her face as she squints her eyes to make out the visitor.

"Shalom, Cousin Elizabeth!" shouts Mary, seeing her at the window. The moment the sound of Mary's voice reaches Elizabeth, she catches her breath and clutches her stomach. The baby in her womb leaps with a jubilant thud. Never before has she felt such movement from the miracle she carries.

Elizabeth rushes to open the door. "Mary!" she cries, flinging wide her arms to welcome her younger cousin. Instantly the Holy Spirit floods Elizabeth and the spirit of prophecy fills her. She stands back, holding Mary's hands and prophesies, "Blessed are you among women, and blessed is the child you will bear!"[2] Weeping, she squeezes Mary tightly and bellows, "Why am I so favored, that the mother of my Lord should come to me?"[3]

Kneeling down, the older woman splashes Mary's dusty feet with warm water, then rubs them with oil and kisses them profusely. Mary can feel the hot tears rushing down her own cheeks. She sighs and throws back her head in sweet relief, laughing and crying at the same time. "Dear Elizabeth, I knew you would understand, but how did you know that I too am with child?"

Elizabeth rises, and with eyes blazing says, "As soon as the sound of your greeting reached my ears, the baby in my womb leaped for joy."[4] She grabs Mary's hands and looks deeply into her eyes. "Blessed is she who has believed that what the Lord has said to her will be accomplished."[5]

Mary sighs and slumps against her older cousin, sobbing like a child in its mother's arms. Elizabeth weeps too, both of them knowing they are caught up together in a master plan which reaches far beyond what either of them can comprehend.

Minutes pass and finally Mary loosens her grip on her cousin. As she straightens, suddenly her heart begins to tremble. She feels the prophetic unction surging like the slow rumble of a volcano, rising and spilling, and ready to overflow from her heart. Still holding Elizabeth's hands, with the spirit of revelation flowing between them, she opens her mouth and cries, her whole body vibrating under the power of God:

> My soul glorifies the Lord and my spirit rejoices in God my Savior, for he has been mindful of the humble state of his servant. From now on all generations will call me blessed, for the Mighty One has done great things for me—holy is his name.[6]

She pauses for a moment, and then continues, her face beaming with light:

> His mercy extends to those who fear him....He has scattered those who are proud in their inmost thoughts. He has brought down rulers from their thrones but

has lifted up the humble....He has helped His servant Israel, remembering to be merciful to Abraham and his descendents forever.[7]

When she finishes, she falls back into Elizabeth's arms, weak and shaking.

The days pass too quickly for Mary. She feels completely at home with Elizabeth and her husband Zechariah. The atmosphere of love and acceptance heals her bruised heart and nourishes her with confidence. She feels so close to God here with the morning prayers, the daily Scripture readings, and the intimate talks which she and her cousin share together.

"What do you think our sons will be like, cousin?" Mary often asks.

"The angel told me, as well as my husband, to give him the name John. He said our son will be 'great in the sight of the Lord.' He will 'go on before the Lord' to prepare the way for Him.[8] Oh, Mary, do you know what this means?"

"Tell me, Elizabeth," cries Mary, hanging on every word.

"Your son will be more than a prophet. He will be the Lord God Almighty, the Son of the Living God, the Messiah, the King of Israel!"

"Yes, yes, that's what the angel told me. He said to 'give him the name Jesus.' And 'he will be great and will be called the Son of the Most High. The Lord God will give him the throne of his Father David, and...his kingdom will never end.'"[9]

Each time they talk of the destiny of their sons, their spirits soar and their hearts are knit together more tightly. They know they are part of a grand tapestry which God has been weaving together in their very wombs, an embroidery that will ultimately cover the earth with a blanket of glory.

The months pass quickly, and soon it is time for Elizabeth's travail. Mary is more than three months pregnant and her own belly protrudes noticeably. With deep regret she knows it is time for her to return to Nazareth. She arranges to join a caravan heading north, and then sadly bids Zechariah and Elizabeth farewell.

As the donkey trudges along the dusty road to Nazareth, worry tugs at Mary's heart. *What will Joseph be like when I return? I had hoped for a visit, or at least a note on parchment, but not a word has come. Will he want to divorce me, since betrothal can only be broken through a legal writing of divorcement? What if he wants me stoned for adultery? Oh, he would never do that! He loves me too much.*

What about my parents? Will they be too ashamed to take me in? If they cast me out I will be left homeless and alone—and what of the baby?

> *Oh, Father, this is Your Son! Please protect Him, protect us and change the hearts of those I love...*

Day after day she wrestles with these tormenting thoughts, while listening to the endless plodding of donkey hooves clicking along the road. Finally, they draw near to the city gate of Nazareth. As they pass the well, the women look up and scowl. "Look, it's Mary....See how her pregnancy shows!" "Poor Hannah and Heli! Such disgrace she has brought to them." "And poor Joseph, betrayed by the one he loves. Why, that girl should be ashamed to show her face in this town!"

Suddenly Mary feels a sharp blow to her temple. Something wet streams down her cheeks. A boy has hurled a stone at her yelling, "Whore!" Then he scampers away laughing. Blood runs profusely down Mary's face. More stones pelt the cart, and she places her hands over her head, ducking her face beneath her prayer shawl. She wails,

God, help me! Protect me from those who don't understand who He is! Nevertheless, Father, I thank You for the honor of carrying Your Son!

When the caravan leader catches wind of the gossip—that he has an unwed pregnant girl among them—he stops the cart and snarls, "Get out!" Cursing under his breath, he mutters angrily, "She can walk the rest of the way! Serves her right!"

Lugging her bag over her shoulder, she slips off the cart and treads wearily up the pathway to her parent's house. When she nears the little hovel, the children playing in the olive grove see her. "Mary's home!" they squeal, surrounding her with hugs and kisses.

Word reaches her parents and they rush to meet her. "Mary, my child! Oh, what has happened to you?" her mother shrieks when she sees the bruises and blood on her face. Running wildly toward her daughter she throws her arms open wide. Then she looks down at her protruding stomach and halts. "Oh, no! Then it's true!" she whimpers, clenching her hands into knots. Her face reddens as she cries bitterly, "Such shame you have brought on us, child!"

"We had hoped it wasn't true," her father groans heavily.

"Have you seen Joseph?" she asks anxiously. At this her parents freeze and look down. The long silence that follows causes Mary's heart to sink. Finally her father clears his throat and says, "His father Jacob says he is preparing to divorce you privately."

"Oh, no!" Mary wails. "How can that be? He loves me and I love him!"

You should be grateful that he doesn't want to publicly divorce you for adultery, which would require a public stoning!" Heli blurts.

"Grateful?" She looks at her parents, her face scarlet, hot tears scalding her cheeks. "Then you, my own mother and father, still don't believe!"

She squares her shoulders and clutches her stomach. With eyes blazing she proudly proclaims, "This child is the Son of God!"

Rushing to the ladder she climbs to the roof, and kneels down on the terrace floor, sobbing. Finally the tears subside and she stares out into the darkness. Slowly a sweet thread of hope weaves its way back into her thoughts...Elizabeth...

There on her cherished rooftop, hope springs afresh as Mary clings to her cousin's words: "Blessed is she who has believed what the Lord has said to her will be accomplished....As soon as the sound of your greeting reached my ears, the baby in my womb leaped for joy."[10]

Yes, Mary, this baby in Elizabeth's womb leapt for joy at the nearness of the Messiah. He didn't just kick or nudge his mother; He jumped inside her when he came near the baby you carry.[11] He was responding to the presence of the Lamb. Indeed, the day will come when Elizabeth's son, John the Baptist, will point to Jesus and thunder—"Behold! The Lamb of God who takes away the sin of the world!"[12] You see, as John leapt in his mother's womb, he was already bearing witness to the glory of Bethlehem's Lamb, even before his birth.

Even today, these five simple words of John the Baptist— "Behold! The Lamb of God!"—hold immeasurable truth for you and me. Whatever weighs you down, behold the Lamb of God.

Keep your eyes fixed on Jesus until everything else fades and healing comes, until joy floods you, and the life of God fills you. For "nothing so clears the vision, heals one's heart, stirs fire in the bones, breathes life in the human spirit, and burns passion into the soul as a long, steady look at God's Lamb."[13] Indeed, we find life in a look at Bethlehem's Lamb.

CHAPTER 3 ENDNOTES

1. It was from eighty to one hundred miles to the hill country in Judea, which took three to four days by foot or caravan (Hughes, *Luke*, vol. 1, 40).

2. Luke 1:42. "There was a strong spiritual joy in the meeting of these two expectant mothers—one in the flower of youth, the other's bloom long gone. These two were to become innocent co-conspirators, soul-sisters in the divine plot to save the lost. They would share their hearts as few humans ever have. Through their birthing pain, sweat, and blood, and their mothering too, the world would receive its greatest blessing" (Hughes, *Luke*, vol. 1, 40).

3. Luke 1:43

4. Luke 1:44

5. Luke 1:45

6. Luke 1:46–49. This song of Mary is called the *Magnificat*.

7. Luke 1:50–55

8. Luke 1:15, 17

9. Luke 1:31–33

10. Luke 1:45, 44

11. "Only a mother can relate to the sensation described here because more than a prenatal kick or turn, it was a leap, an upward vault….Why did Elizabeth's baby react in this way? The answer is two-fold. First, there was a prophet in her womb, and this was his first prophecy….Second, John leapt because he was overcome with the emotion of joy" (Hughes, *Luke*, vol. 1, 40–41).

12. John 1:29 (NKJV)

13. This is a quote from Sandy Davis Kirk, *The Masterpiece* (Hagerstown, MD: McDougal, 2007), 11.

Chapter 4

JOSEPH'S DREAM

A Story of Unfolding Faith

"No!" SCREAMS JOSEPH, sitting up on his pallet, his clothes drenched with sweat, his thin blanket twisted around him. Every time he closes his eyes he sees Mary with another man. Or worse, he sees people hurling stones at her, shouting "Adulterer!" "Harlot!" Since the night she told him those stunning words, "I am with child," he has barely slept.

He flings off the covers and jumps up, restlessly pacing the floor. *Oh, Mary, I can't get you out of my mind! Surely, love drives a man mad,* he thinks. His heart heaves with torment. His fevered brain reels in confusion. *My precious Mary, how could you wound our love so deeply?* He has loved her almost beyond reason, but now all of his dreams of marriage and family have been shattered like a storm-tossed boat dashed against jutting rocks.

How could she betray me like this? I loved her so. I would have given my life for her. She said she loved me too, but now I see it was all a sham. She only wanted a name for her baby.

He throws himself back down on his pallet, beating his fists into his pillow. Waves of darkness sweep over him. Nearly eight months have passed since Joseph has seen her. He knows she has returned from her cousin's home in the hill country, but he hasn't gone near. By now she would be heavy with child. The sight would be revolting, heartbreaking to this grief-torn lover.

He put it off as long as possible, but had finally applied for a divorce a few days earlier. He would divorce her privately to avoid public exposure.[1]

Though he knows Mary has surely endured her own share of humiliation, no one can understand his own private hell. *I've become the laughing stock of Nazareth, the brunt of endless jokes! "There goes the carpenter who's betrothed to a whore," they whisper. But I always know what they're saying. Some even accuse me of being the father. "Joseph just couldn't wait! Now he's too proud to admit it!"*

But worse than the gossip is the emptiness he feels. His heart aches over the loss of his beloved. And though he tries to turn to the Lord in prayer, God seems strangely distant to him these days.

Tossing fitfully, he finally drops off into an exhausted sleep. Suddenly, in a dream, a supernatural presence invades his sleep. He sees a light glowing brighter and brighter, and within the light he hears the voice of an angel. The voice seems almost audible: "Joseph son of David, do not be afraid to take Mary home as your wife, because what is conceived in her is from the Holy Spirit."[2] A profound peace floods his soul as the angel continues: "She will give birth to a son, and you are to give him the name Jesus because he will save his people from their sins."[3]

"Mary! My Mary!" he cries, suddenly awakening, with the presence of God upon him.

Dear God, this baby is from You! I have been so wrong!

He leaps from his pallet, splashes himself with water, throws on his tunic, and races out into the street toward Mary's house.

The orange glow of dawn is just peaking over the horizon as Joseph runs breathlessly up the winding road. A few vendors are already beginning to set up their wares along the street. Several torches still burn restlessly, most standing cold and flameless.

But the flame in Joseph's heart burns strong, fueled by the oil of his love and the grief of remorse.

> *Dear God, I didn't believe her! My precious little Mary, my beloved!*

"Oh, Mary, my Mary!" he cries, tears stinging his blood-shot eyes as he stumbles up the path.

What will I say when I see her? I promised at our betrothal to protect her and faithfully stand with her through all trials, but I walked out on her. I doubted her. How can she ever forgive me? How can she ever respect me as a man when I've been so easily deceived, thinking only of my feelings, and not hers?

When he finally reaches Mary's home, he almost wants to break through the door, but then checks himself. *Where are your manners, Joseph?* he berates himself. He knocks, then pounds on the door, frantically calling her name.

Hannah opens the door cautiously, and Joseph bursts into the little room, breathless and glowing. His eyes search the house for his beloved.

There she stands, kneading dough for the morning meal, ringlets of dark hair hanging over her face. She looks up in shock. Her face looks drawn and pale, frightened by this explosive intrusion. *What does he want? Has his pain driven him mad?* Taking a step back, she flings back her hair and wipes her hands on her apron.

Joseph starts toward her, then freezes, paralyzed by love. He searches her dark liquid eyes, looking for a flicker of love. She looks away quickly, her face blushing, hoping to hide her pain. Her heart feels cold and numb, almost unable to feel anymore. "Oh, my darling..." he finally stammers. He lunges forward and falls at her feet, kissing her hand. "I am so sorry! I doubted your purity. I didn't believe you, and I was so wrong!"

Mary looks at him with an icy glare. She has cried so many tears over this man who she has always loved—who deserted her when she needed him most. Now her heart feels closed. But gradually, as he spills out his love and remorse, her cold heart begins to soften...and finally to melt.

Still kneeling, he looks up into her eyes, speaking with firm resolve, "Mary, this child you carry is from God! The Lord has chosen you to be the mother of the Messiah!"

He pauses and swallows hard, softening his voice. "Mary, He has given me the honor—that is, if you will have me—of being His earthly father. I want you to be my wife, my beloved—if you can forgive me." Then he smothers his face against her stomach and sobs, "Please, please forgive me..."

"Joseph," she whispers, cradling his head, "you are the only man I have ever loved. I do forgive you. I knew the Lord would show you, but I've missed you so desperately!"

His eyes light up and he stands to his feet, folding his arms around her. She falls weak and limp against his chest. "I need you, Joseph," she whispers. "I cannot bear to live without you. I love you more than life itself."

The rest of the household stands back, shocked and silent, as together Mary and Joseph weep in each other's arms. It is as though all the sorrow of the last eight months spills out of their hearts, washing away their pain through the power of forgiveness and the light of their rekindled love.

Finally, Joseph loosens his grip and takes a step back, his face beaming. "I almost forgot, Mary. We must give Him the name of *Jesus*."[4]

"Joseph, how did you know? That's what the angel told me to name Him!"

"He told me, too, my darling—in a dream which was from God."

Heli suddenly breaks in dryly, "How do you know it was a dream from God? Dreams can be from anything." Mary's father had always been a practical man, a student of the Scriptures, and not easily impressed with spiritual experiences. "Only fools follow dreams," he sneers.

"Sir, respectfully I must disagree. This was not just any dream. I went to sleep in torment and pain; I awoke from my dream with a peace like I'd never known. It was the presence of God resting heavily upon me." As he spoke, everyone listening could feel the presence of the Holy Spirit filling the room.

"Even so, I don't believe it!" Heli retorted, shaking his head. Everything in him wanted to believe that what Joseph said was true. Most of all, he longed to believe that his daughter was innocent of adultery. This was his little girl, his firstborn. She has always been his golden one; but all this talk of angels and glory and dreams seemed like nonsense. He once heard of a woman who claimed to be pregnant with the Messiah and it was sheer fantasy, a silly woman's folly. As it turned out, this other woman wasn't even pregnant, and she disgraced her whole family with her fanciful delusions.

Turning to Mary, Joseph says, "Mary, come home with me tonight, and in a few days we will travel together to Bethlehem."

"Bethlehem!" shrieks Hannah. "No, you can't. The time of your travail will be upon you soon. You wouldn't dare be so far from home at such a time."

"We must go, Mary. Caesar Augustus has issued a decree for a census. We must register in the town of our lineage. For both of us it is the City of David—Bethlehem."

Heli gives a sudden gasp and grows very quiet. He strokes his beard as though deep in thought. "Bethlehem…" he mutters with a faraway look on his face. "Bethlehem?"

Then a sudden light flashes in his eyes. He looks at his daughter with shock as though he was seeing her for the first time in months. Silence falls on the room as everyone looks at Heli, waiting for him to speak.

His eyes moisten and his voice softens as he says, "The prophet Micah writes, 'But you, Bethlehem Ephrathah, though you are small among the clans of Judah, out of you will come for me…'" Heli's voice breaks and the tears begin to fall. "Out of you will come for me *one who will be ruler over Israel*, whose origins are from of old, from ancient times.'"[5]

Walking slowly and painfully across the room, he takes Mary's hands and, through chokes and sobs, he quotes Isaiah: "The virgin will be with child and will give birth to a son."[6]

"My daughter," he cries, his face scarlet with contrition, "I believe! This child is the coming Redeemer! He is the eternal Son of God, the ruler over Israel—our long-awaited Messiah!"

He buries his face in her shoulder and sobs, "Mary, I believe! I believe! Forgive me for ever doubting you—my pure and innocent child. The chosen one of God."

Finally, straightening himself, he brushes away tears and clears his throat. Placing his hands on Joseph's shoulders, he says, "Please forgive me, my son, for accusing you and doubting your honor. This child is indeed the Messiah, conceived by the Holy Spirit, and God has chosen you as His earthly father."

Hannah looks on dazed. Then a scream tears from her throat as she rushes to Mary's side. "Oh, my child, my poor child, I too believe! I am so sorry that my pride caused me to be ashamed. I have been so wrong. No matter what the world may say, you have honored this house by being the one chosen to bear the Messiah!"

Turning now to Heli, she wipes her tears and smiles, "My dear husband, do you know what this means?" Her eyes sparkle with delight as she announces—"Our first grandchild will be the Son of God!"

The day is far spent by the time Mary finishes her packing and Joseph loads the borrowed donkey. Kissing the children and hugging her parents fiercely, they leave, arm in arm, walking down to the house which Joseph has lovingly built. From that point on Joseph takes Mary as his wife, just as the angel said, though he has no union with her until after the birth.[7]

In only a few days the journey of a lifetime will begin. They will tread the roads of Galilee and the valleys and hills of Judea toward the City of David. Here the miracle of all miracles will occur as the virgin gives birth to Bethlehem's Lamb.

Oh, precious one, reading these pages, do you see why this is the greatest love story ever told? It's the love of a man and a woman; the love of parents for their child; the love of a mother for her baby; the love of a Father for His only Son; the love of God's Son for you and me. It's the most exquisite love story of all human history, and through this story we too can learn to love.

You see, we are born into this world for a reason. Above all else, we are here to learn to love. May you and I pray for God to enlarge our hearts, humble our pride, and teach us how to love. Only God can show us what this means: "For God so loved…that he gave his one and only Son."[8] Indeed, there is only one way we can truly learn to love. It is through the life that He laid down, the life of His Son—through the sacrifice of Bethlehem's Lamb.

Chapter 4 Endnotes

1. See Deuteronomy 22:23–24.
2. Matthew 1:20
3. Matthew 1:21
4. Jesus is the Greek rendering of the Hebrew name for Joshua. It means Jehovah saves. "The name *Jesus* shouts to the world the heroics of the Incarnation and the cross" (Hughes, *Luke*, vol. 1, 92).
5. Micah 5:2, emphasis added
6. Isaiah 7:14
7. The Bible says, "When Joseph woke up, he did what the angel of the Lord commanded him and took Mary home as his wife. But he had no union with her until she gave birth to a son" (Matt. 1:24–25).
8. John 3:16

Chapter 5

A BABY'S CRY

Birthing the Lamb to this Earth

THE DAY DAWNS clear and crisp and filled with expectancy. Bidding farewell to their parents, Mary and Joseph promise to come home soon. However, although they did not realize it, due to the threats of Herod it will be years before they return.

They travel south, turning east and crossing the frigid waters of the Jordan, and then turn back south along the banks of the river. At night they huddle together by a fire, drawing strength from their God and from one another. To herself Mary thinks, *Papa believes! Mama believes! Most of all, my Joseph believes and we are together at last!*

"Oh, Joseph, I'm so happy!" she sighs, cuddling closer in his arms.

"And I as well, my darling. It's good to be on our own and away from the gossiping tongues!"

Here they are—two people in love—the chief characters in God's great love story. This is a story in which the Author of the book will step into His own tale. The Word will become flesh and dwell among us.[1] God will become human, fully God and fully man. He will make Himself vulnerable to the pain and suffering of humanity. He will discover the feeling of a tear slipping down the skin of His cheek. He will lay down His life as a Lamb; and in so doing, He will conquer sin and death, giving eternal life to all who believe in Him.

But all of this is far beyond the thoughts of Mary and Joseph at this point. They are hoping to arrive in Bethlehem before the baby comes, and their minds are filled with thoughts of the long journey ahead of them.

Each morning as Joseph lifts Mary up to the donkey, her discomfort intensifies. As the donkey lumbers down the road, she can feel its heaving sides. With every jarring step her insides jolt and pull. She holds her stomach as though to protect her baby, while her thighs ache and pain throbs through her body. *I can't tell Joseph how I feel*, she thinks. *He already has enough on his mind. I don't want to worry him.*

Although both Mary and Joseph are filled with joy, the trip is slower and more difficult than usual, for Mary has to stop and stretch and walk. Finally on the morning of the fifth day, they cross into Jericho and enter the hill country of Judea. Now, suddenly and unexpectedly, the roads throng with people, swarming in from the hills and adjoining roads.

I didn't expect such a crowd, Joseph thinks, not anticipating that most of this throng is headed toward Bethlehem to register in the census. Since the scattering of the ten tribes of Israel, the majority of people in the land are from the tribe of Judah.[2] They too will be journeying to the City of David, the place of their lineage.

I have enough shekels to pay for a room at the inn, but what if there's no room? And what if her travail starts? How will I ever find a midwife to deliver the baby in this teeming mass of humanity? Who then will deliver the child?

Joseph's face reddens and his palms, holding the donkey's reins, begin to sweat. *Why didn't I think of these things,* he worries, flushing with shame.

Please, God, help me, he silently screams. *Oh, how I wish Hannah were here!* His face looks drawn and lashed with fear.

"Joseph, what's wrong?" Mary calls, sensing his dread.

"All is well, my darling," he assures, trying to force a smile. "We will be there soon."

They plod along in silence, Joseph's head swimming, his mind trying to think what to do. *If there's no room at the inn, I can't let her sleep out in the open fields. If the baby comes, I can't let her be exposed to the gawking eyes of strangers!*

Suddenly, Mary screams a piteous cry that stabs his heart, "Joseph!" He rushes to her side, where she motions for him to lift her off the donkey. His face blanches as he sees the blanket that she had been sitting on soaked with the waters of childbirth.

He holds her until the contraction passes, then he gently places her back on the donkey. She has been having small contractions for the last few hours, but hasn't said anything. Now she can no longer remain silent.

"We must hurry, Joseph," she cries. "The pains are getting worse."

Joseph's heart races as he steps up the pace, elbowing his way through the crowd, and tugging hard on the reins attached to the exhausted donkey. "My wife is in travail," he cries, hoping for mercy, but the people grunt and shove and pay no attention.

The sun is just beginning to drop toward the western hills as they reach the city gates. Then another contraction comes. But the press of teeming, sweating humanity leaves no room for Joseph to lift his beloved to a place of rest. Enduring the pain on the back of a donkey, Mary pants hard, groaning, and gripping Joseph's hand till her knuckles turn white.

Once the pain passes, Joseph looks above the crowd and spies the inn. He tethers the donkey to a post, promising to return as quickly as possible. Fear grips him as he begs for a room. "Sorry, all full! Now move along, son."

"Please, sir, my wife is in the throes of childbirth! We need a midwife and a private room," Joseph cries desperately. "Too bad, you'll have to sleep in the open field," the innkeeper responds heartlessly.

"What's that?" breaks in the innkeeper's wife, coming into the room and catching the last bit of Joseph's plaintive cry. She looks at him with compassion. His face is strained, streaked with tears and dirt, and his eyes plead for mercy. "Did you say your wife is in childbirth? Abner, come now, we can surely find some place for them to have their baby in peace."

The innkeeper rubs his brow and thinks, "There is a little cave on the hill which we use for a stable. I put some fresh straw in there this morning; if you'll build a fire, your wife will be warm and secluded from the stare of intrusive eyes. You're welcome to bed down there if you can endure the stench."

"Oh, thank you, sir, but we also need a midwife. Can you send one to us? I can pay her whatever she wants."

"Mercy me, son," the innkeeper's wife breaks in. "We would never be able to find a midwife at a time like this. But don't worry; the Lord will be with you. Here are plenty of rags and soap. You'll need them when you deliver the baby."

Joseph's face drains and his mouth runs dry. *Me? Deliver the baby? But I am a man, and I know nothing of these things! And surely, it is not proper for a man to look upon childbirth! Dear God, this is too much for a mere man!*

"Oh, please ma'am, couldn't you help us? I know nothing of these things," Joseph says desperately.

"Sorry, son, our inn is bursting at the seams and the guests are clamoring for my help. But I'll bring some hot water as soon as I can."

"Here, young man, take this torch to light the way, as darkness is quickly falling. You can use it to help start a fire," says the innkeeper, his voice now soft with compassion.

Wiping his brow, Joseph straightens his shoulders and returns to Mary, trying to look confident. "The inn is full, but I found a place, my darling—a warm little cave on the hillside. It will give us the privacy we need."

"But, Joseph, who will help me? I thought we would have a midwife! Oh, I wish my mother were here!"

"Don't worry, my beloved. I will be with you," he says bravely. "And most of all, God is with us!" Another contraction hits her and she shudders in pain, clenching Joseph's strong hand until it passes.

Darkness has fallen by the time they find their way up the winding path to their humble abode on the hillside. The clear sky overhead glistens with starlight, but one dazzling star burns brighter, illuminating the path with streaming, almost supernatural light. It even seems to hover over the cave.

Joseph notices and, pointing toward the star, says cheerily, "See, Mary, God is showing us we are not alone. He is lighting our path all the way."

They enter the cave where Joseph drives the stake of the torch into the ground, illuminating the darkness. He sees a pile of hay lying inside near the entrance. He clears out a spot for Mary and covers it with fresh hay and blankets. Then he lowers her to the makeshift bed. Immediately another pain strikes, and she writhes in agony as though her very bones are opening to give way to this wonderful miracle.

When the pain subsides, he holds up her head and gives her a few sips of water. Then he hurries about, gathering twigs and branches to make a fire. Soon hot flames crackle, warming the cave and transforming it into their own little palace.

For a moment Joseph stares into the mesmerizing flames and prays,

> *Father, I'm beside myself with excitement...and fear. Please help me. I am only a man; I don't know about these things. Please send Your angels to help me in this mighty task, for this is Your Son! Surely You will be with me...and with Mary and the baby. Please help us in this miracle of birthing Your Son to the earth.*

He gazes around the humble little surroundings. The air reeks with the pungent scent of urine and the stench of oxen dung.[3] The flames cast animal shadows against the stone walls of the cave. The cattle and oxen lay peacefully. The donkeys rest quietly. Joseph rises to clean out the manger, which is an animal feeding trough, then fills it with fresh hay.

He sits back down in front of the fire and prays,

> *Oh, Father, Your Son should not be born in such squalor. God's Son is fit for a temple or the chambers of a king, least of all an animal stable.*

Joseph grits his teeth, and to himself he thinks, *I feel so ashamed. I was supposed to provide for Mary and protect her, and all I can give her is a filthy animal stable for her child, a feeding trough for His bed.*[4]

Just then the innkeeper's wife calls out from the mouth of the cave, startling Joseph from his thoughts and prayers. "Here, son, I've brought you plenty of hot water and some nice warm lentil soup. She will need her strength."

"Thank you so much, but couldn't you please stay? My wife is very close to giving birth," he pleads.

"Sorry, son, but don't worry. You'll do fine. The Lord will help you." She turns and hurries back toward the inn.

Joseph's head spins.

Oh, God, help me, please!

Returning to Mary, he smiles, "Darling, here is a little soup for your strength. The innkeeper's wife said you'll need it." He pours some soup into a cup, holds up her head, and tenderly lifts it to her mouth. She drinks it hungrily. He strokes her black silky hair, now matted and wet with sweat. He mops her brow and gently lays her back down on the hay.

"Joseph, I'm frightened," she moans.

"Don't be afraid, my beloved. God is with us. This is His Son, and He will protect you and His little One," he says, still hoping the tremor in his voice does not betray the fear that grips his heart.

Joseph stirs the fire and puts on fresh wood to keep the water hot. Though his stomach twists into knots, he remains outwardly calm, a source of comfort and strength for Mary. Knowing her time is near, he carefully washes his hands with soap and hot water and returns to her side.

He finds her thrashing about in the hay, in the throes of pain. Finally she pants breathlessly, "Joseph, the pains are getting closer now. The time is almost upon us." She tries to say more but the pain is too deep for words. She grips Joseph's hand fiercely and moans.

Another contraction. Then another. "I'm here, my darling," he comforts.

"Oh, Joseph, He's coming!" she screams, half crying, half laughing. Her face contorts and she bears down with all her might. "Ahhh…" she groans, wildly grunting and moaning. With one last thrust against the little bundle within her, she pushes.

Joseph braces himself. He bites his lip and reaches out to guide the little head. He spreads his large hands, now shaking violently. But suddenly all fear fades, and he feels encompassed by peace. It is as though God Himself has come, giving him strength and grace for the greatest challenge of his life.

Now, with the grace of an angel, he guides this red-faced infant out into the world. Suddenly a baby's cry splits the midnight air. Then skillfully, like a master craftsman, Joseph cuts the umbilical cord, tying it on both ends.[5]

"He's beautiful, Mary," Joseph cries, as his trembling hands hold up this tiny, squirming baby.

Mary smiles weakly as she looks at His wet, wrinkled little body. Then He cries again, a loud, piercing, powerful wail. Mary gasps; the baby's cry impales her heart, and she realizes, *This is the first time the voice of God has been heard on earth in over four hundred years.* She closes her eyes, exhausted and happy, thinking of the wonder of God in human flesh.

Yes, Mary, now at last the voice of God has rung through Israel again. Indeed, He whose cry tumbled galaxies into space now cries in His mother's arms. He who sprinkled the universe with gleaming stars now rests in a virgin's embrace. He who gazed into the eyes of His Father God now gazes into the eyes of a teenage Jewish girl.

Oh, it's the wonder of the ages! The glory of the Incarnation, God Himself enfleshed with skin; the Creator has become a created being. He who filled eternity with His glory now fills a baby's flesh. He who made man is made a man. The Infinite has become an infant.[6] The Shepherd of Eternity has become a Lamb.

That God would stoop so low, from the heights of heaven to the lowly depths of a stable, staggers our senses. It brings us to our knees to adore Him with endless praise. It calls forth our highest worship as we honor the One who came down to earth as Bethlehem's Lamb.

CHAPTER 5 ENDNOTES

1. See John 1:14.

2. The name "Jew" comes from Judah. This was the tribe which had been released from captivity in Babylon, most of whom had returned to Israel. While a minority came from other tribes, primarily the Benjamites and Levites, the majority were from the tribe of Judah.

3. "If we imagine that Jesus was born in a freshly swept, county fair stable, we miss the whole point. It was wretched—scandalous! There was sweat and pain and blood and cries as Mary reached up to the heavens for help. The earth was cold and hard. The smell of birth mixed with the stench of manure and acrid straw, made a contemptible bouquet" (Hughes, *Luke*, vol. 1, 83).

4. "Mary gave birth to Jesus, with only Joseph attending her. Joseph probably wept as much as Mary did. Seeing her pain, the stinking barnyard, their poverty,

people's indifference, the humiliation, and the sense of utter helplessness, feeling shame at not being able to provide for young Mary on the night of her travail—all that would make a man either curse or cry" (Hughes, *Luke*, vol. 1, 83).

5. "Trembling carpenter's hands, clumsy with fear, grasped God's Son slippery with blood—the baby's limbs waving helplessly as if falling through space—his face grimacing as he gasped in the cold and his cry pierced the night" (Hughes, *Luke*, vol. 1, 83).

6. "The infinite God who filled all things, who was and is, and is to come, the Almighty, the Omniscient, and the Omnipresent, actually condescended to veil himself in the flesh of a creature....The infinite was linked with the infant, the Eternal was blended with mortality" (Charles Spurgeon, "The Great Mystery of Godliness," *Spurgeon's Expository Sermons*, vol. 3 [Grand Rapids, MI: Baker Book House, 1977], 10).

Chapter 6

BETHLEHEM'S LAMB

Finding the Message in the Manger

THE HILLS OUTSIDE Bethlehem lay quiet and still in the darkness. Shepherds keeping their flocks have drifted off to sleep. Only the occasional bleating of a lamb, the incessant chirping of insects, and the soft cooing of a dove calling to its mate can be heard.

Then—suddenly—explosions of light flood the skies. The shepherds awake, astonished. Glory enflames the sky and bathes each one of them.

Fear strikes each man's heart. They leap to their feet, rubbing their eyes and trembling, amazed by this supernatural sight. The presence of God charges the atmosphere, enwrapping them with mantles of living light. Their blood races; they can barely breathe.

They look on terrified as an angel appears in the midst of the brilliance. With the authority of God, he says, "Do not be afraid. I bring you good news of great joy that will be for all people. Today in the town of David a Savior is born to you; he is Christ the Lord!"[1]

Every shepherd's heart almost stops. They look at one another, unable to speak, dazed, and blinking. "A Savior?" they finally murmur among themselves. "The Christ?" "This means the Messiah has been born, right here in Bethlehem!"

As they stand there dumbfounded, the angel continues, "This will be a sign to you: You will find a baby wrapped in cloths and lying in a manger."[2]

"A manger? How strange to put a baby in an animal feeding trough!" whispers one of the shepherds. But before he can continue, the skies split open and hosts of angels flood the heavens above them.[3] With one glorious sound of praise the angels shout, "Glory to God in the highest, and on earth peace to men on whom his favor rests."[4]

Every shepherd hits the ground, awestruck by God's glory. But then, just as quickly as they had come, the angelic hosts depart and the heavens close. The shepherds slowly stand, shaken and wondering.

"Why would angels come to us?" "Who are we? We are nobodies—mere peasants, the poorest of the poor. Why would an angel bother to tell us about the Savior of the whole world?" they wonder, for indeed none of them are scholars of the Bible. None are experts of the law. They hold no lofty positions. They are the offscouring of humanity, for they merely tend the sheep.[5]

"I think I know why," stammers Moshe, the oldest shepherd among them. Lifting his arm and gesturing toward the surrounding hills, he says, "These hills are where our father David tended his lambs. We are David's descendents and we have prayed and believed with all our hearts for the coming Messiah whom God promised David.[6] The Lord must have seen our hearts and our longing for the Messiah."

"Come on, let's get going into Bethlehem and find this Messiah in a manger!" cries a young man. Grabbing their cloaks and staffs, with a few lambs tucked under their arms for gifts, which is all they had to give, they head down the hill into the town. As they approach the city gates, they see the streets jammed with pilgrims.

But how will they ever find one tiny baby in this bustling mass of humanity? From house to house and inn to inn they search. Then suddenly, the youngest shepherd cries, "Look!" Pointing toward the sky, he says, "That star! See how it hovers over that little hill on the edge of town?"

"Yes, yes!" chimes Moshe. "I noticed a strange bright star while we were out with our flocks. If God would speak to us through an angel, He could surely use a star to lead us. Let's follow it!"

The shepherds hasten up the hillside where they see starlight shimmering down on a cave. As they near the cave, they pause, disappointed. "Oh, it's only an animal stable. This couldn't be the place where a Messiah would be born. No Savior of the world could rest His head amidst the filth and stench of animals!"

Then they remember. The angel said, "This will be a sign to you: You will find a baby wrapped in cloths lying in a manger."[7] Though this hardly seems like the proper place for a Savior to be born, as shepherds, they know that mangers are found in stables. So in one accord they nod and agree, "This must surely be the place of His birth!"

A great hush falls over them as they come to the mouth of the cave. They tiptoe toward the opening and peer in, knowing they are about to witness a miracle. In the silence they hear the braying of a donkey, the bleating of a few sheep. A mouse scurries beneath the hay. And then...the cry of a baby. With eyes wide they gaze into the cave. What they see takes their breath away.

Here He lies, wrapped in rags and cradled in the hay of a manger, just as the angel said. The soft golden light of a low burning fire illumines the cave. A shaft of starlight streaming through an opening focuses all of its light on Him, causing the swaddling cloths to shine like gleaming silver.

Joseph sees the look of wonder on their faces, and he motions them to come inside. Mary stiffens and reaches for her baby. She holds Him close as if to protect Him from these crude shepherds.

"It's alright, Mary," Joseph assures her, smiling knowingly. He tenderly takes the baby from Mary's arms and nestles Him in the manger.

Mary looks on, her heart in her throat, as these ruddy, rawboned, wide-eyed shepherds stoop over the feeding trough and gaze upon the Christ Child. In absolute awe, these rough, scraggly bearded men begin to tremble and weep like babies, as they look into the face of God.

She feels a surge of joy mingled with a stabbing pain, as these calloused men shed tears over her baby. For in her heart she knows that Jesus is not hers alone. He is the Son of God—born to be shared with all the world.

Each shepherd kneels, removing his cap and brushing away tears. Their faces burn with the heat of the glory now filling the cave. Although they cannot explain it, they know they are viewing the Savior of the world. One by one, those who carry lambs lay them as gifts at the foot of the manger.

But these are not just any lambs. These are Bethlehem lambs, born to be sacrificed in the temple. Because the City of David is located only seven miles south of Jerusalem, these lambs, born in the hills of Bethlehem, are born for one purpose: they are born to be taken to Jerusalem and slain for sacrifice.[8]

Mary watches now as the shepherds file silently out of the little cave. Then they rush back into Bethlehem, for they cannot contain the news. In the fields, through the town, on the roads, in the temple where they take the lambs for sacrifice, they tell the good news of the birth of the Savior, for they have seen Him face to face.[9]

These poor, lowly, unkempt shepherds—the last people on earth you would ever suspect—have seen what no man on earth had yet been privileged to see. They have seen the heavens roll open as the glory of God exploded through the skies. They have watched thousands of angels, in glowing array, singing of the glory of Christ. They have even heard the voice of an angel speaking of the birth of the Savior. And though they still carry the filth and stench of the sheep pen, they have been the first to gaze into the face of God.

By the time they return to their flocks on the backside of the hills of Bethlehem, rays of crimson and gold are flooding over the horizon. While the dew-drenched slopes sparkle in the morning light, a new day has also dawned in their hearts.

No longer will their task of tending sheep and birthing lambs for sacrifice seem ordinary. They can't quite explain it, but each man's heart is filled with a fresh sense of purpose. They have been chosen above all other men on earth to be the first to behold God's Lamb. And now God has used them as the first evangelists, for this is a shepherd's calling—to proclaim the good news of the Savior—the glory of the Lamb.

Indeed, the angel, shining in the splendor and authority of God, had said, "This will be a *sign* to you: you will find a baby wrapped in cloths and lying in a *manger.*"[10] You see, the sign was not the angel or the star or the cloths. The sign was the *manger*— the animal feeding trough, for it told the story of Bethlehem's Lamb.

And now the story comes together, for this is all part of God's master plan to offer Bethlehem's Lamb to the world.

Why must God's Son have a manger for a crib? Because a manger is an animal feeding trough, the perfect place for a lamb. Why must He be born in a stable, brought forth among sheep and lambs? Because He is God's Lamb, and a stable is a fitting place for a lamb. Why must shepherds be the first, among all the people on earth, to attend His birth? Because shepherds always attend the birth of lambs. That's their job. It's their calling. And why were these shepherds chosen to be the first evangelists? Because that is their highest calling, to preach the message of the manger—the story of Bethlehem's Lamb.

And most of all, why must He be born in this little town of Bethlehem, hidden among the hills of Judea? It wasn't just because of His forefather David, though indeed this was part of the story. It was, above all, because lambs were born in Bethlehem.

Now the mystery of "why Bethlehem" can be solved, for we see why God chose this little town over all the villages, the towns, and the cities in the whole world.

You see, Bethlehem was near Jerusalem, where the temple was located. Even as young lambs were slain in the temple at Jerusalem, Jesus—the Lamb of God—would be taken to Jerusalem to be slain. That's why—in this greatest love story of all time—Jesus was Bethlehem's Lamb.[11]

CHAPTER 6 ENDNOTES

1. Luke 2:10–11
2. Luke 2:12
3. "A heavenly flash and suddenly the bewildered shepherds were surrounded by angels! 'A great company' is literally 'a multitude'—not fifty, not

150, not 1500—but beyond count. I think every one of God's angels was there because this was the most amazing event that had ever happened in the entire universe. I think the heavenly host stretched from horizon to horizon, obscuring the winter constellations. I like to imagine that they radiated golds, pinks, electric blue, hyacinth, and ultraviolet— maybe some were even sparkling....Job tells us that at the creation of the world 'the morning stars (angels) sang together and all the angels shouted for joy' (38:7). Now the angels again joined voices at the greatest creation of all—the birth of the God-man— perfect sympathizer and Savior" (Hughes, *Luke*, vol. 1, 88).

4. Luke 2:13–14

5. "That the message came to shepherds first and not to the high and mighty, reminds us that God comes to the needy, the poor in spirit. Shepherds were despised by the 'good,' respectable people of that day....The only people lower than shepherds at that particular time in Jewish history were lepers" (Hughes, *Luke*, vol. 1, 87).

6. See 1 Chronicles 17; Psalm 132; 2 Samuel 7.

7. Luke 2:12

8. Every day in the temple at Jerusalem, a lamb is examined before dawn. If it is found to be spotless, it is skinned, and flayed in pieces. Then at the third hour, or 9:00 a.m., the priest climbs the rise of the altar and casts it over the grate. He arranges it back in the shape of a lamb where it is consumed in the flames as a fragrant burnt offering to God. (See Leviticus 1.)

9. "Having seen it for themselves, the shepherds told what had been spoken to them about this Child to all around—in the stable, in the fields, probably also in the Temple, to which they would bring their flocks, thereby preparing the minds of a Simeon, of an Anna, and of all them that looked for salvation in Israel" (Alfred Edersheim, *The Life and Times of Jesus the Messiah* [Grand Rapids, MI: Wm. B. Eerdmans, 1971], 189).

10. Luke 2:12, emphasis added

11. Just like these lambs that are inspected and prepared for the daily burnt offering, one day Jesus would be examined by the priests before dawn. Found to be spotless, He would be flayed by a Roman scourge, and at the third hour, 9:00 a.m., He would be cast down on the altar of the cross. Then, taking the punishment for our sin, He would endure the consuming flames of God's wrath, punishing Him in our place.

Chapter 7

A MOTHER'S LOVE

Beholding the God-Man in Mary's Arms

NFATHOMABLE JOY FLOODS her being as Mary holds her infant God in her arms.[1] She looks into His face, so innocent and pure, and wonders, *Is this the face that once shone so brightly in heaven that seraphim hid their eyes from the brilliance of His glory? Is this the glowing countenance that Adam looked upon when he first opened his eyes at creation?*

Deep reverence sweeps over her as she touches His little mouth and marvels, *Is this the mouth that spoke worlds into existence and summoned galaxies into the universe? Through this mouth did You breathe life into a man?*

And with this tongue will You drive out demons? Will You still wild storms and speak peace to storm-tossed lives? Will Your words heal wounded hearts and shake nations to their roots? Even as Your cries pierce the air at your birth, will these lips cry to Your Father in prayer?

A great surge of love flames up in her heart as she uncovers His tiny hands. She pats her face with His palms, and then holds out a finger, watching Him grip it with His fist. Then she cups His hands in hers and ponders, *Are these the hands that dipped into earth's clay to form the body of a man? Are these the hands that will someday mix spit with clay and re-form the retina of a blind man's eyes?*

Oh, my precious One, will You lay these hands on the oozing sores of lepers and see their skin made clear? Will You hold little children and lay Your hands on them in prayer? Will You wipe a widow's tears when You give her dead son back to her alive?

She holds her infant's feet and presses them to her lips. She closes her eyes, tears clinging to her lashes. *Oh, precious Child of God, are these the feet that once tiptoed over stars and danced over streets of gold? Did they step over quilts of glory as You walked with Adam in the garden in the cool of the day?*

And will these same feet tread the foaming waves of the seas and the dusty roads of our land? Will these beautiful feet stumble and become bruised, and will a prostitute wash them with repentant tears? And though many painful steps lay ahead, will multitudes follow forever in Your footsteps?

Her face aglow, she reaches for a skin of olive oil and pulls back His swaddling cloths. She pours oil into her hands and rubs it over His squirming, wrinkled body. He kicks His feet, gurgling and cooing, and her heart swells with a mother's love.

She wraps Him again and cuddles Him next to her heart. She can almost feel His tiny heart beating next to hers. *Yes, my darling Son, was the chest wherein Your heart now beats once clothed with robes of splendor? Did You lay it all aside to let Your heart come beat within the flesh of this human chest?[2] Did this same heart once swell with joy when You created your first man; and did it break with sorrow when Adam sinned, bringing the whole human race into darkness?*

And when You see the pain that sin has caused in this world, will Your heart beat with heavy strokes of compassion, longing to free them from their grief? Will You ache over prostitutes and drunkards? Will You grieve over lepers and cripples? Will You sorrow over the pompous and proud? Will Your heart flood with so much mercy that You'll break and overflow into broken lives?

Mary snuggles her little bundle near and begins to nurse Him. She looks into His shining liquid eyes, so full of appreciation and love, and feels her heart melt into His. *Oh, my Son, did Your beautiful eyes once look into the face of God Your Father? Did You see adoring angels worshiping around Your throne?*

Did You look into the face of the first man and see Him revel in Your presence? But now, will tears fill Your eyes when You see how burdened we've become? Will You weep for our souls and cry for our pain?

Mary gently looses Him from her and lays Him across her shoulder, patting Him until the air bubbles are released. She smiles to herself, knowing this One in her arms is fully God, yet He is also fully man. He hungers, He thirsts, He sleeps, He wets, He weeps, like any baby boy.

Yes, now He who holds all things together by the word of His power, the Almighty Omnipotent One, lies helpless in a mother's arms. The Omnipresent One, who fills all things with Himself, now lies contained in the skin of a baby. The Omniscient One, who knows the beginning from the end, only knows when He's hungry and sleepy and wet.

His beauty almost steals her breath away. Tears swim silently down her face, as she drinks in the beauty of her slumbering child.

Oh, look at Him, Mary. He is the container of everything good. In Him all the attributes of God come together, for in Him "mercy and truth are met together; righteousness and peace have kissed each other."[3] Indeed, in Him "all the fullness of the Deity lives in bodily form."[4]

Mary lifts up her baby to God with a heavy sigh,

Here He is, Father! Here is Your beautiful Son!

Tears run down her cheeks as she continues,

Are You proud of Him? This is the One who carries Your blood rushing through His veins; who carries Your glory flooding through His being; who carries Your power filling His heart and soul. I know You love Him even more than Joseph and I do, so please take care of Him!

Joseph slips over and kneels beside her, his heart too full to speak. He places His arm around Mary and listens to her prayer.

Oh, Father, thank You for this high privilege of carrying your Son. No greater honor could ever have befallen me.

She reaches over and takes Joseph's hand, pressing it to her lips.

Thank you, Father, for these strong hands. Though he felt so incapable, these hands guided Your Son safely into the world. Thank You for my beloved Joseph and the love we share together. May the home we provide for Your Son be filled with the love You would want for Him. Oh, how I pray that Joseph and I can protect Him from what lies ahead!

But, Mary, you cannot protect Him from His destiny as the Lamb, for in Him are treasured up the "unsearchable riches of Christ."[5] But rich treasures must be mined. This is why, like buried treasure, His earthen vessel must be dug open to release the hidden gold. Like a jar containing rich perfume, He must be broken open to pour out His sweet fragrance.

Yes, little mother, He was born to break so that the broken could be healed. He was born to weep so that mourners could rejoice. He was born to be cast out so that outcasts could be brought in.

He was born to bear guilt so that the guilty could be made blameless. He was born to bleed so that sinners could be cleansed. He was born to be punished so that we could be forgiven. He was born to bear hell so we could experience heaven. He was born to die so that the dead can truly live.

So hold Him while you can, for all too soon these precious hands you now hold will claw the ground at Gethsemane and grasp the spikes that hold them to a cross. This pure and innocent Son of God will drink down every drop of the cup of eternal wrath, taking our punishment for sin.[6]

This little heart that pumps the blood of God will pump out, through the wounds carved into His flesh, every last drop of His blood. These soft little feet will be twisted and nailed to the wood, but they will crush the devil's head and triumph over the kingdom of darkness. A soldier's spear will pierce His side and a great ripping will tear open His heart; but as this sacred blood rolls out, it will hold the power to transform the world. It's the power of the blood of the Lamb.

Indeed, this little heart will beat again. These eyes will gleam with love, and flame with glory. For though He was born to die, He was ultimately born to rise and to shine and to pour out the power of Bethlehem's Lamb.

So even now, my dear reader, won't you look up at Jesus on the throne? Let the power of His blood cleanse you, and let the fire of His love come upon you. Even as Mary looked into His eyes, look into the eyes of Jesus. See love beaming like sun rays from His eyes and soak in His goodness.

Drink in His presence, like a sponge in warm water, and let Him saturate every pore of your being. For this is all part of God's eternal plan. He desires to fill up His children, to infuse His whole church, and to flood the whole earth with the glory of Bethlehem's Lamb.

Chapter 7 Endnotes

1. Jesus is fully God and fully man. This is known as the *hypostatic union*, the union of God and Man, the merging of the divine with the human (Wayne Grudem, *Systematic Theology* [Grand Rapids, MI: Zondervan, 1994], 558). "For in Christ all the fullness of the Deity lives in bodily form" (Col. 2:9). "Jesus is the 'theanthropos,' the 'God-Man.' Jesus person is undivided. He is fully God and fully man in one, undivided person" (Allen Hood, *The Excellencies of Christ: An Exploration into the Endless Fascination of the God-Man* [Kansas City, MO: Forerunner, 2006], 26).

2. And yet He "being in very nature God, did not consider equality with God something to be grasped, but made himself nothing" (Phil. 2:6–7). This self-emptying of the Son of God is called the *kenosis*,

meaning that He gave up the independent exercise of His transcendent attributes and was completely dependent on the Father and the Holy Spirit.

And what an incredible self-emptying this was! Samuel Rutherford said that "he would like to pile up ten thousand million heavens upon the top of the third heaven to which Paul was caught up, and put Christ in that high place; and then he would not be as high as he deserved to be put; and truly, no honors seem sufficient for him who stripped himself of all he had that he might become the Saviour of sinners" (Cited by Charles Spurgeon, "Christ's Crowning Glory," *Spurgeon's Expository Sermons*, vol. 13 [Grand Rapids, MI: Baker Book House, 1977], 380).

3. Psalm 85:10 (KJV)
4. Colossians 2:9
5. Ephesians 3:8
6. For a heart-gripping view of the cup, see my book *The Glory of the Lamb* (McDougal, 2004) and *The Unquenchable Flame* (Destiny Image, 2009).

Chapter 8

MARY'S PIERCED HEART

The Bittersweet Pain of Carrying the Father's Lamb

THE OLD MAN shuffles up the narrow cobblestone streets of Jerusalem, his long white hair flowing in the breeze. Friends stop and wave, but he hardly notices. His eyes flash and his face burns, for his heart is fixed on getting to the temple.

Today I will see the consolation of Israel. The Messiah. I know I will see Him today! he thinks as he hurries toward the Temple Mount. He has waited his whole life for the promise of the Messiah to be fulfilled. Now at last the highlight of his life, the moment for which he has prayed and longed and ached, has arrived.

As he nears the temple, the white marble columns and gold engravings shine brightly in the morning sunlight. He hobbles up the massive stone steps, feeling an unusual spring in his normally aching limbs.

His heart hammers in his chest with heavy strokes as he enters the Court of the Gentiles. Here the loud clamor of money

changers, the bleating of lambs, and the sounds of other animals
and birds can be heard; but all he can hear is the thundering of
his own heart pounding in his ears.

He hastens through the Court of the Women, his cheeks
flushing hot with the spirit of revelation. He elbows his way
through the crowd—looking, searching, longing.

Then suddenly he halts, arrested by the Holy Spirit. He feels
the trembling rising from deep within. His hands shake. His eyes
burn like torches. *That's Him,* he thinks, spying a young Jewish
girl holding a baby on the inner steps.

Mary has been waiting on these steps in the inner court,
holding the baby Jesus in her arms, for what seems like hours.
She watches as the priest lifts up the slivers of lamb's meat for the
morning's burnt offering. At last the priest turns to her. Joseph
takes the baby, while she hands the priest two pigeons, which is
the offering of the poor.[1]

The priest cuts the birds' throats and sprinkles their blood
upon her, declaring her clean from the contamination of
childbirth. Then Mary hands him five silver shekels to redeem
the firstborn.[2] The priest pronounces the benediction and she
descends the steps. Smiling and looking up, she whispers under
her breath,

> *Oh, Father, if only this priest could see what a paradox
> this is! Here I am paying the redemption price for the
> Redeemer of Israel Himself!*

Simeon, the old prophet, stands back reverently, watching
and waiting until the purification is completed. He too knows
the irony of this situation, as the Redeemer Himself is being
redeemed. Then with his heart still pounding wildly in his chest,
he approaches Mary and reaches out his arms for the child.

His abruptness startles her. She flinches back, shielding her baby. But when she sees his sparkling eyes and the glory blushing on his face, she knows the Spirit of God is upon him. Darting a glance toward Joseph, she cautiously hands the child to Simeon.[3]

Lifting Him up, the prophet shouts with a voice as strong as any young man's—"He is 'a light for revelation to the Gentiles and for glory to your people Israel...This child is destined to cause the falling and rising of many in Israel.'"[4]

Mary's heart lurches. *What could this mean*, she wonders. But then the old man turns and looks deep into Mary's eyes. Solemnly he says, "And a sword shall pierce your own soul too."[5] Strangely, Mary can feel these words driving sharp and deep, like the quick thrust of a blade, into her sensitive being.[6]

However, before she can give these words any serious reflection, a beautiful, white-haired old woman named Anna, from the tribe of Asher, rushes up to her.[7] With her face glowing like a sunrise, she carefully pulls back the fringes of the blanket snuggled around the baby's face. Suddenly she breaks into ecstatic praise, overjoyed at seeing her Messiah.

For over sixty years Anna has fasted and prayed for her Messiah, living in the temple since her husband's death.[8] Now she has seen Him face to face and she knows she has found her greatest purpose in life. She spends the rest of her days telling everyone who longs for His coming about the "redemption of Jerusalem."[9] In "whispers and with bated breath," she tells them of the glory of Bethlehem's Lamb.[10]

By the time the little family finally heads back to Bethlehem the sun dips low, bathing the hills with hues of deep purple and violet. As she rides on the back of the donkey, holding Jesus close, Mary thinks about these strange encounters in the temple: the prophet with his declarations of glory and heart piercing; the beautiful old woman who looked into His face and reeled back in awe.

She feels a strange throbbing inside, like a wound pulsing and aching in her soul. She recalls again the words of Simeon the prophet, "And a sword shall pierce your own soul too."[11] She has felt this ache before.

Mary thinks of the pain of rejection she felt from her parents, the wounded love of her beloved Joseph, the gossip of the people in Nazareth, the lonely trip to visit Elizabeth, the painful birth in the filthy animal stable, the strange visit from the shepherds, and especially this morning when the prophet spoke to her of the sword that would pierce her soul.

She realizes that with each new revelation of Jesus as the Lamb, she has felt a fresh jab of the sword. Strangely, an Old Testament verse floods her mind. Her heart sinks as she recalls, "He was led like a lamb to the slaughter, and as a sheep before her shearers is silent, so he did not open his mouth."[12]

She clutches her baby closer and lifts her heart in prayer.

Oh, Father, what does this all mean? What will my son—Your Son—have to endure?

Even as she prays she can feel the blade of the sword twisting inside.

But it is a bittersweet piercing, mingled with pain but filled with sublime purpose beyond her highest dreams. A great tide of love sweeps over her and revelation fills her heart. She feels so close to God, to His heart, that she can almost sense what He must have experienced when He tore His Son from His side.

Gratitude overwhelms her as she thinks of the Father's sacrifice.

Thank you, Father, for being so vulnerable, for laying your heart bare and taking the risk to let Him go.

She wonders out loud to God,

What was it like when Your Son bid His last farewell to You? Did You hold Him and weep, never wanting to let Him go? Did You follow Him to the edge of Eternity, holding on to every last visage of Your Beloved? Did it wrench Your heart when He slowly and painfully shed His garments of glory, then walked out of Your glorious throne room and into a virgin's dark womb? Did You reach for Him and long to retrieve Him, Your heart aching to hold Him again?

How could You do it, Father? I will never understand. To expose Your beloved Son, who never knew hate, who never touched sin, who never felt pain or grief or rejection? I know I've borne rejection myself, but it pales in comparison to the rejection He will bear. Oh, thank You, my Father, for tearing open Your heart, and letting Him come. Thank You for the honor of bearing Your Son and birthing Bethlehem's Lamb into this world!

Yes, Mary, and when His work on earth is done, and He rises back to His Father's throne room, there the Father will stand, His arms outstretched in waiting. The Son will run back into His Father's arms as together they weep in each other's embrace.

And when their tears subside, the Father will lift His mighty arm and point toward His Son. With love bursting from His heart, He will proclaim through time and eternity—"Behold the Lamb of God...slain from the creation of the world!"[13]

And just to be sure we never forget, there beyond the veil, seated on the throne, still bearing wounds from His sacrifice, there stands "a Lamb, looking as if it had been slain."[14] Over and over again, God shows us His Son as the Lamb, ever reminding us of the greatest love story of all time—the story of Bethlehem's Lamb.

Chapter 8 Endnotes

1. "The more wealthy brought a lamb for a burnt offering, the poor might substitute a turtle-dove, or a young pigeon....The substitution of the latter for a young lamb was expressly designated 'the poor's offering'" (Edersheim, *Life and Times*, 195–196).

2. "And now the priest once more approached her, and sprinkling her with the sacrificial blood, declared her cleansed. Her 'firstborn' was next redeemed at the hand of the priest with five shekels of silver" (Edersheim, *The Temple* [Grand Rapids, MI: Kregel, 1973], 222).

3. "Simeon surely held the baby tight. It would have been impossible for him to do otherwise given his ecstasy. He looked at Jesus—and looked—and looked again. His heart overflowing with joy at the coming of the Redeemer and the fulfillment of God's personal promise to him, soared even beyond his song" (Hughes, *Luke*, vol. 1, 96).

4. Luke 2:32, 34

5. Luke 2:35

6. "This prophecy would become very important to Mary. In her *Magnificat* she sang of how the future generations would call her 'blessed.' But here she learns that the future will also bring great sorrow. That future would include the family's flight to Egypt, her Son's being misunderstood and rejected, the terrible events of Passion Week, and watching her Son die on the cross....A great sword would go right through this mother's soul! The most honored woman of all would know great pain" (Hughes, *Luke*, vol. 1, 97).

7. Alfred Edersheim said that women from the tribe of Asher were unusually beautiful, often fit for a king or a high priest (Edersheim, *Life and Times*, 200).

8. Luke 2:36–37

9. Luke 2:38

10. Edersheim, *Life and Times*, pp. 200–201.

11. Luke 2:35

12. Isaiah 53:7

13. John 1:29; Revelation 13:8

14. Revelation 5:6

Chapter 9

THE FATHER'S HEART

Loving Bethlehem's Lamb at Christmas

N THE TINY yard outside a little house in Bethlehem where his family now lives, Joseph busies himself sawing boards for a baby bed. He takes a step back to survey his work.

Suddenly he hears the crunch of hooves coming up the road. He looks up to see a strange procession of camels with lavishly dressed princes astride. Perhaps they are wealthy merchants, or even kings; he doesn't know, but he can't imagine what business they would have in this part of Bethlehem.

"Excuse me, Sir," interrupts one of the men. "We are Magi from the Far East and have been following a certain star." Pointing upward he says, "We have come to see the child who is a King. Would you happen to be His father?"

Joseph's heart leaps to his throat. He stands up tall, clenching his fists. Edging over in front of the door of his house, he takes a protective stance.

"Sir, we have come to bring gifts and to worship the King of the Jews," said another, his eyes bright with hope.

Joseph hesitates, the tension easing. "Let me tell my wife," he says. Quietly opening the door he finds her nursing the child. "Mary, some men, Magi from the East, have come to bring gifts, they say, to the King of the Jews."

Mary smiles knowingly. "Let them in, Joseph," she says, covering herself. "They must have come from far away and are probably tired and cold."

Joseph steps back out and invites them in. He watches the men, dressed in rich brocades and silks, tapping the necks of their camels. The massive animals fold their legs and crouch as they dismount.

Reverently they enter the little hovel as the sound of swishing silken robes and the fragrance of exotic perfumes drifts through the humble little dwelling. Joseph looks at them warily, but relaxes when he sees the looks on their faces as they fix shining eyes upon the face of the child. One by one the Magi remove their jeweled turbans and fall to their knees before Him.

A hush of wonder falls over them. The first Magi lays his treasure chest full of gold before the little one. "For the Prince of Glory," he says radiantly, "for He is the King of all kings!"

The next one, swarthier in complexion, places a gem-covered jar of rich incense at His feet. "For the One whose fragrance will fill the whole earth," he whispers reverently.

The last one hesitates, his throat tight with emotion. He gently lays down a vase of liquid myrrh. "For His death," he softly sighs, barely able to speak, "for He has been born to die for a fallen human race!"

A fresh twist of the sword turns in Mary's heart as she hears these words, for she knows that myrrh is used to embalm bodies. Then the sword cuts deeper as she hears the warning of the Magi. "You must leave Bethlehem immediately! Herod's jealousy has been aroused and he will seek to kill Him before His time."

They quickly depart, mounting their camels. Joseph watches and wonders. *They have left everything*, he thinks, *their homes, their families, and their country, to seek the Messiah. And now they have brought this foreboding news about Herod. I must comfort Mary or she will be beside herself with worry.*

The Magi tap the necks of their camels, signaling them to rise from their crouching position. Then they ride off into the night.

"Oh, Joseph, what did they mean?" Mary's mind swims with confusion and fear. "Our child must be in danger!"

"I don't know, but let's try to get some sleep. I'm sure the Lord will show us what to do."

That night Joseph awakens, trembling and soaked in sweat. "What's wrong, my love?" Mary asks sleepily, sensing his fear. Then she feels his glistening body, wet with perspiration. She sits up abruptly. "What is it, Joseph?" she cries, her voice quivering. "Something must be terribly wrong!"

"My darling, we must leave immediately, just like the Magi said. In a dream I saw the angel and heard him say, 'Get up...take the child and his mother and escape to Egypt. Stay there until I tell you, for Herod is going to search for the child to kill him.'"[1]

A muffled scream breaks from Mary's throat. She falls against Joseph's side, knowing her worst fears are becoming a reality.

"Quickly, Mary. Our son is in danger! We must gather a few belongings and leave right now!"

They arise and leave hurriedly, Joseph leading the donkey with Mary and the child on its back. Even now, as they head south on a back road to Egypt, they can hear the sound of horses hooves thundering down from Jerusalem toward Bethlehem. Already swords are being drawn for the blood bath soon to take place in Bethlehem. Tragically, all little boys under two years old will be slain—the first martyrs for Jesus Christ.

Soon Herod will die and the little family will return to their hometown in Nazareth.[2] But Mary doesn't know all this yet; fear grips her whole being as she clutches her child tightly.

> *Oh, Father, I'm so afraid, but this is Your Son! Please protect Him from Herod's jealous rage. I know You will, for You love Him even more than I love Him.*

Suddenly a surging tide of love and faith swells up within her. She thinks of her love for the Father, her love for her son, her love for Joseph. In the last few years she has learned to love like she never dreamed she could. But she knows what she must do, for the very nature of love involves sacrifice. It means giving. Love requires giving up her own desires for a cause higher than herself. She sighs heavily, for she knows love must be willing to give up this child of her heart to a higher purpose. For the sake of love she must be willing to relinquish her son to His high calling.

She can feel the Father's heartbeat pounding in her heart. His love pulses through her veins. Since the night when the glory came down on the rooftop in Nazareth, she has felt so close to the Father's heart. It's as though they share a mutual bond, a profound secret, a love for this child that no one else can fully share. Through all her sufferings, she has felt Him near, His warmth and understanding, always causing hope to shine through her tears.

> *Father, no one understands like You. This is Your Son, not even mine. You've only given Him to Joseph and me for a short time in the span of His life.*

As she prays, she can feel the Father's heart trembling with love for His one and only Son.

A vast tenderness flames up again in her heart. She breathes out heavily and looks up to heaven. With all the passion of her soul she cries,

> *Oh, Father, this is Your Son! I give Him to You, to Your great destiny for humanity.*

She presses her little boy closer, soaking Him with her tears, and continues,

> *Father, Your unselfish love astounds me. You gave the deepest part of Your heart that we who are dead might live. This is a sacrifice beyond comprehension. Such love is beyond me. Now I want to live my whole life bringing glory to You for the gift of Bethlehem's Lamb!*

And so may it be with you and me, for no greater gift has ever been given. Indeed, "God so loved the world that He gave His one and only Son, that whoever believes in Him shall not perish but have eternal life."[3]

Yes, from the bowels of eternity, God ripped open His heart and gave His Son as a Lamb. Of all the titles of Jesus, this is the one dearest to His heart because it tells the whole story—from glory to glory, from before creation to His exaltation back upon the throne, from eternity past to eternity future, He was and is and will ever be God's eternal Lamb.

This is why in Revelation, which is a window into heaven, John only describes Him as the "Lion" one time,[4] the "Word of God" one time,[5] the "King" three times,[6] and the "Morning Star" one time.[7] But he describes Him as a "Lamb" in twenty-nine verses.[8] The Father never wants us to forget the colossal sacrifice

He made when He tore His Son from His side and gave Him as a Lamb on a cross.

Listen to heaven's highest worship and you will hear angelic hosts continually singing, "Worthy, worthy, worthy is the Lamb!" They are amazed that God would bend so low, coming in human flesh as a Man and then giving Himself as a Lamb. Angels don't worship Him for His miracles, His teachings, His power, or His resurrection glory. Their song tells it all: they cry, "Worthy is the Lamb" [9] because He was slain, and with His blood He purchased men for God. May our worship be like heaven's worship, continually honoring Bethlehem's Lamb.

So this year, let's make Christmas different. We've let too many Christmases slip by without truly honoring and loving the Lamb. Let's love Him like we've never loved Him before. Let's worship like we've never worshiped Him. Let's love family and friends as we've never loved them before. Let's give like we've never before given.

And with our hearts inspired anew by the courage and love of a teenage Jewish girl, let's carry this message in our hearts. Let's bring back to the center of Christmas the greatest love story of all time.

But more importantly, let's bring the Lamb back to the center of Christianity. Even as He stands "in the center of the throne"[10] above, let's bring Him back to the center of the throne of His church on earth. There He stands—shining with love and blazing with glory. He's God's greatest gift to humanity, and especially to you and me. May we live our whole lives, like Mary, bringing honor and glory to God for the gift of Bethlehem's Lamb.

Chapter 9 Endnotes

1. Matthew 2:13
2. Matthew 2:20
3. John 3:16
4. Revelation 5:5
5. Revelation 19:13
6. Revelation 15:3; 17:14; 19:16
7. Revelation 22:16
8. The twenty-nine verses about the Lamb in the Book of Revelation are 5:6; 5:8; 5:12; 5:13; 6:1; 6:3; 6:5; 6:7; 6:16; 7:9; 7:10 ;7:14; 7:17; 12:11; 13:8; 14:1; 14:4; 14:10; 15:3; 17:14; 19:7; 19:9; 21:9; 21:14; 21:22; 21:23; 21:27; 22:1; and 22:3.
9. Revelation 5:12
10. Revelation 5:6

FROM THE AUTHOR'S HEART

I F YOU HAVE been touched as you've read this little book, would you allow me to share with you my heart behind Bethlehem's Lamb? For me, the story goes back to a Methodist Sunday school class in Texas more than twenty-five years ago. This was my first time to tap into the feelings of the Father for His Son.

The class was discussing the purpose of the Lamb and His Cross. I had been studying the crucifixion for a "Life of Christ" course I was teaching. Through the writings of one of America's greatest theologians, Jonathan Edwards, I had been reading about the Father's cup which Jesus prayed about in the garden.[1] As I read, my heart was completely undone by the magnitude of His sacrifice.

Although I was only a visitor that day, I finally could stay silent no longer. I opened my heart and poured out about the cup of punishment which Jesus engulfed in our place on the cross.[2] As I spoke, I could almost feel the Father's heart aching for His Son. The trembling started somewhere deep inside and soon my whole being was shaking with the presence of God. My face burned with the heat of His glory and my words carried a fire like I'd never known. I could sense the Father's heart trembling with love for His Son.

When I finished speaking, the class begged me to come back

and tell them more, which I did. But what wrecked me was what I felt from God. It was as though He had opened heaven and I could feel His heart burning down upon me. It was a fire like I'd never experienced in my whole life. I had been Spirit-filled for years, but never had I experienced such fire and glory and power as I did that morning. I had struck a raw nerve in the heart of God and my soul vibrated with the pulsations.

I sat in church, tears rolling down my face, my body trembling under the power of God. I promised God that for the rest of my life I would teach and write and study and preach the Lamb and His cross. Like Paul, I resolved "to know nothing…except Jesus Christ and him crucified."[3]

From that day forward I studied the Lamb, the cross, and the Father's cup. I began writing books and pouring out a message of the glory of the Lamb. For the next fifteen years I tried to find a publisher, but no one was interested. Once a publisher looked me in the eyes and said, "You make me sick!" I had graphically described the wounds of Jesus on the cross, and he was repulsed by a sight of His blood.

Book rejection after book rejection followed. I felt like Mary: I was pregnant with a message of the Lamb, but no one wanted it. No publisher took interest in my books and no people cared to listen. Even as there was no room for the Lamb in the inn, there seemed to be no room for the message of the Lamb.

During this time I finished a PhD at Fuller Theological Seminary, where most of my studies focused on the theology of the cross. Then I began pouring out the message to my students in ministry school, and everything changed. It honestly surprised me, but I found that when students of all ages gazed deeply at the Lamb, the cross pierced their hearts like a sword. Most of them flamed with an undying passion for God. I soon found that this is what this pain-wracked, disillusioned, often fatherless generation needs. They need a vision of Jesus that burns like a fire in their hearts. They need something real, something raw; something they could die for so they can truly live.

Soon I was seeing students weeping on the floor of my classes, the carpet of our chapel, the dirt floors of Africa, cement floors in Peru or Hong Kong or Taiwan. Their hearts were being ravished—undone[4]—by a revelation of the Lamb. This is now my ninth published book about the Lamb, and I pray it has touched your heart.[5]

My critics were quick to say, "There's no new revelation of the Lamb!" I always wanted to respond, "I never said it was new. It's as old as the Bible. This is simply an unveiling of Jesus as God's Lamb which is weaved throughout all of Scripture." Because the positive response from students was so overwhelming, sometimes jealousies arose, trying to discredit the message of the Lamb. But I could feel the heartbeat of God, always urging me to never give up. I still felt a bit like Mary, carrying the Lamb and burning with the Father's heart for His Son. Though the church seemed to emphasize blessings and prosperity and every other subject, I could feel the Father thundering for His Son to be honored on earth for His sacrifice as the Lamb.

Bob Sorge says, "I am persuaded there is nothing God feels more strongly about than the cross of His Son....Never has anything torn and lacerated the infinite depths of God's heart as deeply and severely as the crucifixion of His beloved Son. And He'll never forget it."[6]

The reason He'll never forget it is because in heaven—and this is what causes my heart to stand still—the Father gazes continually on His wounded Son![7] There He stands, deep holes and gashes still carved into His human flesh. Now the Father ever beholds Him as glory bleeds from every wound.

This is what touches the tender nerve in the heart of God, for *this is His one and only Son!* How do you think the Father feels when He looks at the raw wounds of His beloved Son,[8] whom He tore from His side and sent down to earth, so that we could have eternal life? And how do you think it makes Him feel when He sees the Lamb relegated to a back corner of the basement in the church, only remembered once a year at Easter?

We are called "the wife of the Lamb";[9] we are invited to the "wedding supper of the Lamb";[10] we overcome Satan by "the blood of the Lamb";[11] and our names are written in the "Lamb's book of life."[12] How then can we neglect to honor the Lamb? The Father looks down upon this earth and thunders—"It's time for My Son to be honored as the Lamb on earth as He is honored in heaven!"

So as you come to the end of this book, I pray that this story— the greatest love story of all time—has inspired you to live for this one sublime purpose. Not just at Christmas, but all year long. Inflamed by love, may you live your whole life to bring Jesus, the Lamb who was slain, the reward of His suffering for you. No higher vision can lead you. No loftier ambition can fulfill you. No greater dream can compel you. This is your highest calling. It's life's greatest purpose—to live for Bethlehem's Lamb.

Now, as you lay this book aside, I must share one final story. When I was a child, I desperately wanted to know God, but my parents were atheists. I made them drop me off at church, but I still couldn't find God. I didn't know that, if I truly wanted to know God, the One who was born in a manger must be born in my own heart. Finally, when I was thirteen, someone told me more about Jesus and led me in a prayer to confess my sins and to pray to receive Him. I repented deeply and He forgave me and came to live in my heart. I was overjoyed because for the first time in my life I really had a relationship with God.

If there could be just one person reading this little book who has never prayed to receive Jesus, why not make this Christmas the greatest of your life by praying to receive Him now? Tell Him you are genuinely sorry for your sins, name them to Him, and then open wide your heart and ask Him to come inside. He will come in and give you a whole new life. He will fill you forever with the love of Bethlehem's Lamb.

From the Author's Heart Endnotes

1. References about the cup which Jesus prayed about in the garden: Matthew 26:39, 42; Mark 14:36; Luke 22:42; John 18:11

2. Jonathan Edwards described this cup as "vastly more terrible than Nebuchadnezzar's furnace." It was indeed "a furnace of wrath into which he was to be cast." Edwards said that Jesus' "principal errand into the world was to drink that cup" ("Christ's Agony," *The Works of Jonathan Edwards*, vol. 2 (Edinburgh: Banner of Truth Trust, 1995), 867–868.

3. 1 Corinthians 2:2

4. My next book, coming out in 2012, is entitled *Undone…by the Glory of the Lamb*.

5. For a graphic and heart touching view of the Lamb and the cross, see my books *The Glory of the Lamb* (MacDougal, 2005), *The Masterpiece* (MacDougal, 2007), *The Unquenchable Flame* (Destiny Image, 2009), and others.

6. Bob Sorge, *Power of the Blood* (Kansas City, MO: Oasis House, 2008), 3.

7. John saw Him as a wounded Lamb in twenty-nine verses, thus how much more does the Father see Him as a wounded Lamb? John only had glimpses; the Father sees Him continually. Again these twenty-nine verses about the Lamb in the book of Revelation are Rev. 5:6; 5:8; 5:12; 5:13; 6:1; 6:3; 6:5; 6:7; 6:16; 7:9; 7:10 ;7:14; 7:17; 12:11; 13:8; 14:1; 14:4; 14:10; 15:3; 17:14; 19:7; 19:9; 21:9; 21:14; 21:22; 21:23; 21:27; 22:1; and 22:3. It is also important to note again that John saw Jesus described as a "Lion" one time (Rev 5:5); as the "Word of God" one time (Rev 19:13); as a "King" three times (Rev 15:3; 17:14; 19:16); and as the "Morning Star" one time (Rev 22:16), but He is described as a "Lamb" in twenty-nine verses.

8. When Jesus presented Himself to His disciples, He showed them the wounds in His hands, and feet, and side. A week later He showed Thomas His wounds. It was important to Him that we know He still bears wounds in His flesh. The reason He looks like a slain Lamb in heaven is because He carries wounds like a sacrificial lamb.

9. Revelation 21:9

10. Revelation 19:9

11. Revelation 12:11

12. Revelation 21:27

ACKNOWLEDGMENTS

I WISH TO PAY special tribute to Marjorie Holmes, a great Christian author of our day. Though I never took her classes, I read her books and learned from her how to carve feeling and emotion into writing. Her novel *Two from Galilee* first inspired me to realize that Joseph and Mary would have loved each other dearly. She said, "God, who loved us enough to send his precious son into the world, would want His son to be raised in a home where there was love—genuine human love between his earthly parents."[1]

She went to be with Jesus on April 1, 2002, but she left behind a score of wonderful Christian books. I've read her books through the years and have been continually inspired by her craftsmanship as a wordsmith. She brings biblical narrative alive with her rich descriptions and tender emotion weaved into the characters of her novels. I honor her for the impact she has had on my Christian life and writing.

I also want to thank my friends and students who read the early pages of this manuscript and encouraged me to finish this book. It didn't seem to be as spiritually deep as my other books, so I was a bit unsure about going forward with it. Mary Wells, her mom, Susan Clay, Rebecca Garner, and Dawn Jackson were my greatest encouragers. Thank you so much to these, some of my dearest friends, for your help.

For several nights with my daughter and later with some of my students, I gathered them into my cozy bedroom and read them the story. I especially wanted to see if the "childbirth" chapter could pass their sensibilities. Having given birth to twins and attended the births of my grandchildren, the story of birth seems beautiful to me; but to some it can be quite gruesome. After much healthy and hilarious debate, I decided to edit out a few details, while still being rather graphic about the birth of Jesus.

When the book was done, my faithful friend Cathy Ovenshire read it and wrote several beautiful Christmas songs, placing them on a Christmas CD entitled "Bethlehem's Lamb." It perfectly flows with all that is written here.

I wrote this book over a period of three years, laying it aside and then picking it up at Christmastime to see how I felt about it. Not until I added the genuine feelings and emotion did the story come alive. I wanted so much to give Mary a proper Jewish wedding, though it would have been hurried and small. But I wanted to stay true to Scripture and the Bible says, "When Joseph woke up, he did what the angel of the Lord had commanded him and took Mary home as his wife."[2]

So I offer this story to you with the prayer that it has made your Christmas a little brighter this year. In the years to come, I plan to gather my children, grandchildren (when they are old enough), and students around the fireplace at Christmastime to read them this story. I hope you'll do the same. I pray it will enkindle for you and those you love an unforgettable awareness of the glory of Christmas.

—Sandy Davis Kirk
America Ablaze Ministries
Lillian, Alabama
January, 2011

ACKNOWLEDGMENTS ENDNOTES

1. Marjorie Holmes, *Two from Galilee* (New York: Bantam Books, 1986), vi.
2. Matthew 1:24

ABOUT THE AUTHOR

Dr. Sandy's heart burns to bring Jesus, the Lamb who was slain, the reward of His suffering. She is a theology professor, leading "Glory of the Lamb" and "Revivalists of the Cross" Internships at a beautiful camp on the Gulf Coast. She teaches in Bible colleges and churches and ministers with a team of "young revivalists" throughout America, England, Kenya, and East Africa, as well as Canada, Hong Kong, and Germany. She has written eight other books. She earned her PhD at Fuller Theological Seminary in Pasadena, California.

CONTACT THE AUTHOR

CALLING "REVIVALISTS OF THE CROSS"

Spring, Summer, or Fall

Twelve-Day or One-Month Internships

Participate in this one-month Internship at Camp America Ablaze on the Gulf Coast where you will receive a deep impartation of the Cross, and the Fire of Revival.

CONTACT:

Website: www.gloryofthelamb.com

E-mail: drsandy.aam@gmail.com

Phone: 251–979–9068

OTHER BOOKS
by DR. SANDY KIRK

America Ablaze

A Revelation of the Lamb for America

The Glory of the Lamb

Rivers of Glory

The Cry of a Fatherless Generation

The Pain

The Masterpiece

The Unquenchable Flame